NINE YEARS AMONG THE INDIANS, 1870–1879

LATEST PHOTO OF HERMAN LEHMANN

NINE YEARS
AMONG THE INDIANS,
1870–1879

THE STORY OF THE CAPTIVITY AND LIFE
OF A TEXAN AMONG THE INDIANS

HERMAN LEHMANN

EDITED BY J. MARVIN HUNTER

FOREWORD BY DALE F. GIESE

UNIVERSITY OF NEW MEXICO PRESS

ALBUQUERQUE

First published by Von Boeckmann-Jones Company, 1927.
Foreword © 1993 University of New Mexico Press.
All rights reserved.
First paperback edition.

Library of Congress Cataloging-in-Publication Data
Lehmann, Herman, 1859–1932.
 Nine years among the Indians, 1870–1879 : the story of the
captivity and life of a Texan among the Indians / Herman
Lehmann : edited by J. Marvin Hunter : foreword by Dale F.
Giese. — 1st pbk. ed.
   p.   cm.
 Originally published: Austin, Tex. : Von Boeckmann-Jones Co.,
[© 1927]. With new foreword.
  ISBN 0-8263-1417-1 (paper)
  1. Lehmann, Herman, 1859–1932.   2. Apache Indians—
Captivities.   3. Apache Indians—Social life and customs.
4. Comanche Indians—Social life and customs.   5. Texas—
Biography.   I. Hunter, J.
Marvin (John Marvin), 1880–1957.   II. Title.
E99.A6L44   1993
973'.0497—dc20   93–3032
                                                      CIP

DEDICATION

TO THE YOUNG PEOPLE OF MY COUNTRY,
THAT THEY MAY KNOW
HOW THEIR PARENTS AND GRANDPARENTS LIVED,
AND THE UPS AND DOWNS THEY AND THE
INDIANS HAD TOGETHER, THIS BOOK
IS RESPECTFULLY DEDICATED
BY THE AUTHOR

CONTENTS

CONTENTS

FOREWORD

Dale F. Giese

Most historians agree that *Nine Years among the Indians, 1870–1879: The Story of the Captivity and Life of a Texan among the Indians* by Herman Lehmann is one of the very best captivity narratives ever published on the Apaches and Comanches. J. Frank Dobie called it "the finest of the captive narratives of the Southwest."

Herman's story was originally published in 1899 by Johnson Brothers Printing Company in San Antonio, Texas. Written by Judge Jonathan H. Jones of Mason County, Texas, it carried the cover title *Indianology*. The description on the title page read:

A Condensed History of the Apache and Comanche Indian Tribes. For Amusement And General Knowledge. Prepared From The General Conversation Of Herman Lehmann, Willie Lehmann, Mrs. Mina Keyser, Mrs. A. J. Buchmeyer And Others.

The 1899 version, very rare today, differs from *Nine Years among the Indians*, which was published by Von Boeckmann-Jones Company of Austin, Texas in 1927. First, Willie Lehmann, Mina Keyser, and Mrs. A. J. Buchmeyer do not appear to be participants in the latter work. Second, although Herman dictated both versions with honesty and humor, the 1927 story is more carefully edited than *Indianology*.

For more than twenty years I have used the Lehmann-Hunter story in my university classes as a primary source of Plains Indian life as seen through the eyes of this remarkable man.

Herman's story is about a young boy born of German immigrant parents who lived near Fredericksburg, Texas. At the age of eleven he was captured by Mescalero Apaches and eventually gained warrior status. Because he killed an Apache medicine man five years later, he was forced to flee for his life. Joining the Comanches voluntarily, he continued his Plains Indina way of life until Quanah Parker convinced him to return to his mother in Texas. He does so reluctantly, adapting with much difficulty to an industrialized society.

Herman relates that the Apaches and Comanches operated in bands and rarely came together in a large body. He further states that all bands had some white and Mexican captive children. In the course of his narrative, he mentions many of their names. Continuing to reflect on his life, he says, "My career has been rather checkered; I have lived as a savage and as a civilized man, and while I love my old Indian comrades, the refining influences of civilization have brought a great change in me. When I was a savage I thirsted to kill and to steal, because I had been taught that that was the way to live; but I know now that that is wrong. I would not take human life now, nor would I steal."

Through Herman's eyes we learn of the role of Indian women, who performed all of the labor except the making of weapons and pipes. While the birth of a male brought much rejoicing and meant a future warrior, the birth of a female received little attention. He notes that illegitimate children were rare among the Native Americans and that if a married woman committed adultery, the penalty was to cut off her nose.

Male slaves such as Herman were highly prized, for they meant additional warriors for the tribe. In a relatively short period of time, Herman was undergoing a warrior training program that taught him how to ride, fight, manufacture bows, arrows and shields, and poison arrows. He seemed to learn quickly and soon grew to love his Indian comrades and their way of life. Later he would have several opportunities to leave and rejoin his family in Loyal Valley, Texas, but he preferred the society of the Apache people. Only after a drunken brawl, during which he killed a medicine man in self defense, did he escape the Apaches— to save his life. Instead of returning to his family, he

FOREWORD

chose to become a Comanche and continue the life style of the Plains Indian warrior.

Of particular interest to students and scholars is Herman's ability to humanize Native Americans, who are neither noble nor bloodthirsty savages in his narrative. For instance he describes incidents in which they made careless, comical, and tragic mistakes. On one occasion they were caught bathing by the Texas Rangers, who took all of their horses and killed several warriors. At another time one brave accidentally shot himself in the knee, and at still another one of Herman's people out hunting antelope killed a warrior who, dressed as an antelope, was also stalking the prey. Peace and harmony did not always reign among the plains tribes. At times the Comanches and Apaches joined in mutual alliances against the whites, and sometimes they desperately fought each other. Some Apache bands even warred on one another. Alcohol, "hoosh," was often the underlying cause. There was great hatred of the Tonkaways, who had allied themselves with the whites. Herman graphically describes the cannibalism they practiced on the Comanches.

The subject of religion is one that Herman clearly came to view from both the white and Indian perspectives. Of one raid he relates, "Down near Smoothing Iron Mountain we took twenty-five horses, tore down fences and left things like we believed the Great Spirit had intended them to be, free and open. . . . if the Great Spirit had wanted the country to be enclosed He would have fenced it." Herman and his Indian companions believed in an afterlife and often buried their comrades with their weapons and buffalo robes, and horses and servants. The latter were killed for this purpose. On the subject of worship, he speaks frankly: "I have seen just as much earnestness and less hypocrisy among the Indians in their worship as I ever have since I came among the whites. . . . I am glad God has spared my life and permitted me to live to see these wonderful changes. I gave reverence to Him in the only way I knew how when I was an Indian; I worship Him now after the manner of an enlightened white man."

Hatred of the whites is one of the dominant themes in Herman's story. He quoted Victorio as saying, "'The white man is the Indian's enemy, and the Indians must quit fighting among themselves and all go together to fight the palefaces. While I was gone I saw as many palefaces as there are sprigs of grass on the plains or stars in the sky, and if we continue to fight each other we will all be exterminated by the white man.'" Herman mentioned that the plains were overrun by buffalo hunters who were killing the animals for their hides. He saw thousands of carcasses of buffalo, which "made us desperate to see this wanton slaughter of our food supply." He says, "Our men were getting scarcer everyday, war parties and raiders would go out and never return. We held a great council, in which other tribes participated, and pledged ourselves to kill all of the whites as they came into our territory; kill them as they destroyed our game; kill them as they slew our warriors; kill them as they killed our squaws and children; to follow them and kill them so long as any of us remained, and on the break-up of the council we had a big war dance."

The buffalo hunters were not their only targets. Cowboys and the cattle industry came in for their share of enmity. Apaches and Comanches stole Texas cattle, which they sold to the Pueblo Indians in the Rio Grande Valley. Herman said,

The Pueblos lived in Mexico and on the border land, were great traders, spoke the Mexican language, had their own herds and would pay a good price for cattle. . . . We would often get biscuits, sugar, coffee, meal and flour, besides guns and ammunition. . . . We could send by those fellows for almost anything we wanted (but that was usually mescal or whiskey) and they were faithful to their promises but we never paid for anything until we got it. The credit system was not in vogue among our tribes.

FOREWORD

Fort Bascom, built near Tucumcari, New Mexico in 1863, was constructed to deter or halt both this exchange and another, the comanchero trade. Mexican traders brought onto the Southern Plains a quantity of goods to trade with the Apaches, Comanches, and Kiowas in return for horses, mules, and cattle stolen from Texas ranches. Herman and his companions were involved in this trade. He records that "we journeyed southeast and met a large party of friendly Mexicans with pack burros well laden with flour, meal, coffee, sugar and little trinkets to trade to the Indians for horses and mules, and they camped with us several days." The Mexicans sometimes joined the Indians on these raids. In one incident, he recalls, "One time a party of Mexicans came to our camp to trade with the Indians. They had plenty of mescal, corn whisky [sic], and tobacco, and most of the tribe got drunk. One hundred and forty of the Indians and sixty of the Mexicans went on a cattle raid, and west of Fort Griffin, on the old trail, we ran into a big herd being driven to Kansas."

At another time Herman recounted how the Apaches and Comanches met Mexicans on the plains to trade their horses for sugar, meal, sun-dried biscuits, guns, ammunition, whiskey, and mescal. Sometimes they would swap ten horses for one gun and once gave twenty horses for one needle gun. So

vital was such trade to the Indians that wearing
Mexican scalps on his belt brought the warrior little
honor.

In time, the buffalo hunters were almost everywhere on the Southern Plains. Herman relates that
many of them were wealthy sportsmen, "green" from
the states, who were armed with the finest weapons
and an abundance of ammunition as well as being
outfitted with first-class camp equipment. Thus, the
Indians kept themselves well supplied with the property of these hunters. Some they killed, others they
spared. One individual mentioned in the 1899 version
was captured, robbed, and stripped. Then each warrior struck him one time as he ran the gauntlet to his
escape. He was made to promise that he would move
his camp and try to keep the whites out of the territory. Just the same, more and more people came,
and ranches and forts were established everywhere.

As Herman's band of Apaches and then Comanches
moved throughout Texas and into parts of New Mexico, they were in constant search of food. This consisted of bison (his buffalo), horse, mule, cattle, bear,
antelope, deer, peccary, wood rat, dog, skunk, pos-
sum, and lice (especially after a buffalo hunt). According to Herman, wild mustangs were captured by
creasing: "shooting an arrow into his back just behind
the shoulders; too low or too far back would cripple or

kill. It takes a good shot, but we were adepts [sic] at that." Herman noted that his people used dogs for hunting and protection and that a Newfoundland had once successfully protected a child from wolves.

Religion was very much a part of hunting. In the 1899 version, Herman says:

> The Apache was ever mindful of the great Creator and stood in awe and reverence before all nature and the handiwork of God. He had no idea of Christianity but he bowed to every weed that he bent, every stream that he crossed and begged the pardon of every animal that he killed and always praised or emplored the Great Spirits after each chase, engagement or war.

At one time Herman gambled using cacti with different numbers of specks on them in a game of craps. Another time the Indians bet heavily on the ability of their comrades to rope antelope from a fleeing herd. Saddles, blankets, horses, and guns changed hands, and Herman became one of their favorites to bet on. He mentioned that it was the warrior's religious duty to pay his gambling debts.

In his introduction to the 1927 edition, J. Marvin Hunter referred to the fact that Herman married a "splendid" girl in Loyal Valley and later went to live in Indian Territory on a Comanche headright given to him by the federal government. In the 1899 version Herman included a chapter titled "Work, Wedlock and Things Worse." He spoke of jobs he held around Loyal Valley, quarreling and drinking. He "loved beer and other strong drinks, and when a man did anything I didn't like, I never quarreled with him. But I would knock it out with him; . . ." Eventually he asked a Miss Burks to marry him, and she agreed. Although her father approved, he did not think the marriage was a good one because of his daughter's terrible temper. Herman loved his first wife very much, but in time she would prove unfaithful. He related, "I had only five dollars in money but I saddled and straddled my pony and rode back to the Comanches at Fort Sill, and spent several weeks with Quanah Parker." After several months he decided to return for his cattle, which he had left in Loyal Valley. He found his wife with another man, and at this point, he says, "I carried her to her mother and told her that I would rather be separated than live with such a woman. Several hard words passed but I left her there never to see her again."

After the separation Herman bought a team and wagon and began freighting. He continued to drink and fight; so the Methodist Church decided to expel him from its congregation. He gambled, raced horses, made money fast, and spent it just as fast. In

FOREWORD

Cherry Springs, Texas he operated a saloon and made easy money, but according to Herman, he became too fat and drank too much. He sold the saloon and soon spent all the proceeds. The only mention of his second wife by Herman comes from his statement, "I have now found a good woman for a helpmate, have two bright little boys to make our home cheerful and I'm scratching in the soil for a livelihood."

Through this wonderful narrative Herman brings to us the story of a lad uprooted from his family and thrust into a totally alien culture, but a lifestyle exciting for a teenager. He grew to love these people, and they shared mutual feelings for him. We gain more than just insight into the Indian way of life. Through Herman's eyes we really come to understand just how they lived, fought, and died. Herman tells their story just as he lived it among these, his, people. Their story becomes his story with all of its violence, hardships, humor, passion, and love.

INTRODUCTORY

Herman Lehmann, with whom this book has to deal, was born of German parents, June 5, 1859. He was captured by a band of Apache Indians when he was about eleven years old, and lived with this tribe for four years; later he became involved in difficulties with members of the tribe and was forced to flee for his life. He went out into the wilderness, where alone in the mountains he remained for about a year, and later he went to the Comanches, into which tribe he was adopted, and he remained with them until he was finally restored to his people, being grown at the time of the restoration, and to all intents and purposes a wild Indian. During his captivity he had forgotten his mother's tongue, had abandoned the white man's ways, was a blood-thirsty, thieving savage, and when brought back to civilization he had to be forcibly restrained to keep him from slipping away and going back to his tribe. In time, however, he became reconciled, re-civilized, and eventually made a good citizen.

I have known Herman Lehmann personally and intimately for thirty-five years. When he was brought back from his captivity my father, the late John Warren Hunter, was living at Loyal Valley, the home of Lehmann's mother, and I have heard him relate amusing incidents of Lehmann's Indian ways, and how the savage boy would scare the children of the village. My own mother used to tell me if I was not good "that Indian" would sure get me. For a long time he dressed in his Indian garb; he did not like the white man's clothing; he wanted to be alone, out in the woods; he kept aloof from everyone for a long time after his return. Finally, as the refining influences of a mother's undying love, the cheerful associations of a happy family circle, and the affectionate treatment by his brothers and sisters, brought about a complete change in this wild character, and the wildness gave way to a kind and noble nature, and he became a white man again. But he never forgot his friends, the Indians. Years afterward, after he had married a splendid girl at Loyal Valley, he was granted a headright in the Indian Territory, through a special act of Congress, and he went there to live upon his claim, and among his tribe. Yes, his tribe, for he was still a Comanche in the eyes of his copper-colored brothers, and he still possesses all of the tribal rights and privileges even unto this day.

In giving the story of his life in this volume, I am giving it just as he gave it to me, without exaggeration, without boasting, and only in the hope that the reader will find it interesting and a true recital of facts. There are people living today who know all of the circumstances surrounding his capture and re-

turn; there are Texas Rangers who know of his partic-
ipation in battles with the Rangers; there are Indians
who went on the warpath with him, and fought by his
side in bloody conflict.

Herman Lehmann is an old man now; his long and
eventful life is nearing its close. He feels the weight of
years, but he can look back into the far and dim past
without regrets over any overt act he may have, in
the savage state, committed, because, as he says, he
was taught by the Indians to steal and to kill. He
believed it was right. After his restoration he soon
learned that it was wrong to do these things, and he
has not done them. His conscience is clear, and he
believes that a just God has pardoned him for whatever sins he may have committed in savagery, when
he knew no better.

Some thirty years ago Judge J. H. Jones of Mason
published a book, "Indianology," which dealt at
great length with the captivity of Herman Lehmann,
and from this book I have obtained valuable material
which is used in this volume. But most of the facts
were related to me by the ex-captive, who, at this
date, May 28, 1927, is with me and telling me of his
harrowing and hair-raising experiences.

J. MARVIN HUNTER.

NINE YEARS AMONG THE INDIANS, 1870–1879

CHAPTER I

MY CAPTIVITY

My father and mother came over from Germany with the Prince Solms Colony in 1846, and settled at Fredericksburg, Gillespie County, Texas. My father, Maurice Lehmann, died in 1864. Mother married Philip Buchmier in 1866. Some time after the war they secured a large tract of land on Squaw Creek, about twenty-five miles northwest of Fredericksburg. On this land they built their frontier cabin and engaged in farming on a small scale, and stock raising.

From the beginning of the Civil War and up to 1872 the Indians made their periodical raids into Gillespie and adjoining counties, extending their depredations as far south as Austin and nearly to San Antonio, and the sod of many of the smiling valleys had been encrimsoned with the blood of these hardy pioneers while endeavoring to establish in the wilderness a home for their families.

The valleys of Beaver Creek and Squaw Creek and their tributaries offered an inviting field for the daring pioneer, and two or three other German

1

CHAPTER I

families located near our ranch, and these, although several miles apart, formed the nucleus of a small settlement. The soil along these valleys was exceptionally fertile; springs abounded, timber was plentiful, the range was excellent, and there was plenty of game. With these natural advantages and despite the raids of the Indians, during which numbers of horses were driven off and our cattle maimed and slaughtered, the colonists prospered beyond precedent, and today their descendants are among the most prominent in point of intelligence and wealth of all the citizens of Mason and Gillespie Counties.

One day, in the month of May, 1870, I, with my brother, Willie Lehmann, and my two sisters, Caroline and Gusta, were sent out into the wheat field to scare the birds away. Gusta was just a baby at the time, probably two years old, and was being cared for by Caroline. I was about eleven years old, Willie was past eight years old, and Caroline was just a little girl. We sat down in the field to play, and the first thing we knew we were surrounded by Indians. When we saw their hideously painted faces we were terribly frightened, and some of us pulled for the house. Willie was caught right where he was sitting. Caroline ran toward the house, leaving the baby, and the Indians shot at her several times, and she fell, fainted from fright. The Indians had no time to dally with her, so they passed on thinking she was dead, and they often told me she was killed, and I believed it until I came home several years later.

They chased me for a distance and caught me. I yelled and fought manfully, when the chief, Carnoviste, laid hold upon me, and a real scrap was pulled off right there. The Indian slapped me, choked me, beat me, tore my clothes off, threw away my hat—the last one I had for more than eight years—and I thought he was going to kill me. I locked my fingers in his long black hair, and pulled as hard as I could; I kicked him in the stomach; I bit him with my teeth, and I had almost succeeded in besting him and getting loose when another Indian, Chiwat, came up. Then Carnoviste caught me by the head and the other Indian took hold of my feet and they conveyed me to a rock fence nearby, where they gave me a sling and my face and breast plowed up the rocks and sand on the other side. I was so completely stunned by the jolt that I could not scramble to my feet before the two Indians had cleared the fence and were upon me. They soon had me securely bound upon the back of a bucking bronco, stark naked. The Indians lost no time in getting away from there,

CHAPTER I

and as we raced through the brush and undergrowth, my flesh was pricked and torn by mesquite
thorns and catclaws, and the sun blistered my naked
back and limbs. Death just then would have been
a relief to me. My brother, Willie, was in the same
distressing predicament as I, but he murmured not.
The Indians passed down near Loyal Valley and
on to Moseley's Mountains, where they located some
horses in the valley. All of the Indians, except
Carnoviste, who remained to guard us two boys,
went for the horses, and while they were gone we
heard some shots fired. Carnoviste went out to a
point to ascertain the cause of the shots, and Willie
and I tried to run away, but Willie was unable to
run fast and Carnoviste soon caught us, beat us,
gagged us so we could not scream, and threatened
by his countenance and actions to torture us more
if we made another attempt to get away.

Soon the Indians returned with the stolen horses,
and from there we turned west and traveled for a
ways, and the Indians picked up a gray and sorrel
horse; one had William Kidd's brand and the other
Mr. Stone's. We then turned northwest, passed
by the Keyser ranch and on to the Llano River. At
the river they took us from the ponies, tied me
securely and hobbled Willie, and then all lay down
to rest. They neither made a fire nor ate anything

here. We had had nothing to eat since breakfast that morning. Late in the night we were aroused and set out up Willow Creek, passing to the right of Mason, where the band scattered. Willie and I were separated, he being taken with one party and I with another. The Indians sent back scouts to see if we were followed, and to cover up our tracks if possible.

Carnoviste had me with him. We found a young calf lying down. He made signs for me to catch that calf, using about the persuasion you would to a dog. I was afraid not to obey him, so after the young bovine I went and caught him. Carnoviste jumped down, cut the calf's throat, cut it open, plunged his knife into its stomach, got out the soured milk contents, and ate that nasty stuff with a relish that was sickening to see. I turned away disgusted and sick at the stomach. He made signs for me to eat some, but I made signs that I could not and would not. He grabbed me and soused my head into that calf's paunch and rubbed that nauseous stuff all over my face, in my eyes, up my nose, into my ears and forced some down my throat. He held my nose and made me swallow, but the stuff would not stay on my stomach, and I vomited copiously. He then cut out the kidneys and liver and compelled me to eat some of them while they

5

were warm with the animal heat. I would vomit the mess up, but he would gather it up and make me swallow the same dose again, and again I would vomit. He would soak it in the warm blood and make me swallow it down again. The blood settled my stomach, and I finally retained the revolting filth. Then Carnoviste took me to a hole of water, washed my face, put me on the horse with him, and we went to rejoin the other Indians of our party.

CHAPTER II

WE TRAVEL ON

After traveling some distance we went up on a hill and made a big fire, and soon discovered six Indians approaching with a large bunch of stolen horses. They approached cautiously, and when they discovered our identity they came up and we sat down to a hearty meal of raw and barbecued bull. The other six Indians, who had Willie with them, had gone farther north. We destroyed as much as we could the signs of our camp, sent back scouts, and proceeded on our way northward. There was water all along the way, but I was not allowed to drink, although I was real thirsty. Again we scattered, Carnoviste taking charge of me. He took the loads out of his pistol and gave it to me to see if I knew how to shoot. We played with the weapon for some time, and I began to think the old boy was a pretty jolly companion, although I could not exactly understand him, and then he would beat me.

Suddenly all of the band came together again, twelve in number, and after a consultation they again divided in two parties. Six went west; I was in that company. Six went north; Willie went with them. That afternoon our party stole nine more horses. We came together again, and traveled together until we came to a muddy pond, full of bugs and laden with the essence of frog. We dismounted, and the Indians pulled up a lot of nice clean grass, spread it over the water and used it as a strainer. I went off a little way from the Indians, threw myself on the ground and began to suck up the muddy water through the debris, and was enjoying the cool, refreshing breeze that was then blowing, wetting my palate, and thinking of home, when stealthy old Carnoviste came up to me, soused my head into the mud, and every one of the red rascals laughed at me.

From this water hole we went north, and about 4 o'clock in the afternoon we killed a steer and made a fire on a hill. The Indians were very careful what kind of wood, and also the quantity they used, lest the smoke ascend in too great a cloud, and thus reveal to the white people our presence. Carnoviste staked his horse, and taking me with him, went back some distance. He had a sort of mirror made of a bright piece of steel (the other scouts also had similar mirrors); this he used to throw the reflection of the sun in a certain manner. These signs were signaled from one to another way back the line, and an answer that all was well came. Carnoviste motioned to me, but I did not under-

stand what he wanted. I went a little way and
came back. He motioned and growled again. I
went again and returned. He got mad, drew his
pistol and pointed it at me, but still I could not
understand what he wanted me to do. He lowered
his pistol and started toward his horse. Then I
knew he wanted me to get his horse for him, and
when I brought the animal he threw me up, and
jumped up in front of me and we went to join the
Indians on the bank of a small stream. Willie was
there. There they washed and dressed our sores
and painted us up like Indians, after which they
placed us on horses for a long ride. The forked
stick Indian saddles were not very comfortable to
us by any means, as we were naked and these saddles more than tortured us. The reader can imagine the sufferings of a child who had up to a day
or two before been tenderly cared for by a kind
father, loved by a devoted mother, cut off from all
hope of recovery, not knowing but that each moment was to be the last, his face blistered by the
scorching sun, the skin peeled off his back and
breast, his feet and hands tied, and where he had
rubbed against the saddle (forked sticks) the meat
was worn away nearly to the bone. Could the sufferings of Job have been greater?

CHAPTER III

WILLIE'S ESCAPE

With a drove of horses we were traveling northwestward, and on the fifth day after our capture, while near Lipan Creek, we ran into a party of Rangers while they were dismounted at a water hole watering their stock or preparing to camp. We were not discovered by the Rangers, and the Indians hastily withdrew and turned back the way we had come, leaving the drove of horses, and lit out at top speed. One of the Indians was walking, because he had a sore leg and it pained him to ride. This Indian jumped on the horse which Willie was riding, and followed the other fleeing Indians. The horse began to show signs of giving out, when this Indian threw Willie off into some brush, and continued his flight after his comrades. He urged the horse on for some distance, when the poor animal fell exhausted, and another Indian went back and took him up behind him and they came on.

When Willie realized that he had been abandoned by his captors he got up and wandered around until he came to a plain road, and he traveled this road for a mile or two. He met a man on horseback, who talked awhile to him and then rode on, leaving the little fellow there. Going on further he met a man in a wagon loaded with freight and going to Fort McKavett. This man took Willie as far as Kickapoo Springs, where there was a stage stand, and he left Willie there until he could return and get him. The stage from Fort Concho to Fredericksburg and San Antonio came by while Willie was there at Kickapoo Springs, and the driver wanted to take Willie on home, but the little fellow had promised the freighter that he would wait for him, and in a day or two the freighter returned, got him and took him home to his almost frantic mother. He was gone from home about nine days, and his return was the cause of much rejoicing on the part of the distracted members of our family, who feared they would never see either of us again.

When Willie met the man on horseback near Kickapoo, the boy evidently presented a ludicrous appearance, being painted as an Indian and decorated with a cap made from the scalp of a calf's head which the Indians had put on him, and being of a very timid nature he did not talk much to the man. When he left him, and when, a little further on, Willie saw the freight wagon coming, he mustered up more courage, took off that calf's head cap and threw it away, and hailed the wagoner with confidence, and they at once became good friends.

After we had run for many miles, they keeping me in the lead, the Indians finally halted and held a pow-wow, and as they had lost their herd of horses they decided to go back down into the settlements and get some more, as it would not speak well for them to go back to the tribe without some stolen horses. Accordingly, ten of the number took the back trail, while two Indians, Chiwat and Pinero, agreed to take me and pull for the Indian headquarters, somewhere to the northwest. I was still tied on the horse and riding very uncomfortably, and as we rode forward my thoughts were of my little brother. I did not know what had become of him, and I feared our captors had killed him. I wept bitter tears, and oh, how lonesome I felt, and I yearned to know what had happened to him. Something seemed to tell me he had escaped, but how on earth could he, just a little boy eight years old, ever hope to find his way so far back home across that howling wilderness? And I thought of home, my happy home, and of my dear mother and my little sisters. These unhappy thoughts occupied my mind during the weary hours as we rode along, and I was downcast and sad.

CHAPTER IV

INDIAN TORTURES

We went out above Fort Concho, and traveled three days and nights without sleep, water, or anything to eat. About dark on the third evening (my bonds having been loosened by Chiwat) we came to a little creek and stopped there, and I slipped away and crawled right down into the water. I was so dry that I wanted to feel the water, and I drank and bathed in it for some little time. Soon the two Indians missed me and began to search, but they never thought of looking in the water for me. They finally gave up the search and went on. By that time I had my thirst thoroughly quenched, and I began to think of what I should do. I knew I could never find my way back home; the wolves and wildcats and other wild beasts would certainly tear me up and devour me, and perhaps if I followed the Indians they would see that I did not want to leave them and would probably treat me better. So I hurried on after them. They soon looked back and saw me and waited for me to overtake them. Pinero grabbed me by the hair and lifted me on the horse, and we rode on until about 9 o'clock that night, when we made camp.

The Indians usually selected a high place for their

CHAPTER IV

camp, and being refreshed to some extent by the bathing and water, I observed how they made their fire. Chiwat took two sotol sticks and rubbed them together until they began to smoke. This is done by cutting little notches in the sticks and putting sand on the sticks to cause friction when rubbed together rapidly. After getting the fire started my red companions lighted cigarettes and covered the fire in order to keep it alive and keep the flames down. Then they caught me, tied a rope around my neck and fastened the other end to a bush, strapped my arms behind me, and tied my feet together. This done they secured a pole, each end of which was placed in a forked stick driven into the ground, these forked sticks being about six feet apart. To this pole I was suspended, face down, my arms and feet being tied to the pole. I was so near the ground that my breast barely touched the sand, and the least pressure would draw the cords deep into my flesh. Not content with placing me in this extremely painful position, those red devils placed a heavy stone on my back, pressing my face and nose into the sand, and there I was compelled to stay all night long, with no covering except that large rock on my back. I suffered all of the agonies of death, but when I would groan one of the Indians would jump up and pull my hair and ears, and beat

BILLY CHIWAT, APACHE
Who participated in capture of Herman Lehmann.   Still living.
Aged nearly 100

me. How I lived through that awful night I do not know. About daybreak next morning Pinero removed the rock, unbound the cords, and then drew his gun on me. Chiwat strung his bow and fitted an arrow, and they motioned for me to get up. I did not care if they killed me, for I was willing to die right there, but after several attempts I rose to my feet. I was so sore and stiff I could not stand at first. I was a perfect scab, and a little moving about soon made the worst sores run, and the corruption and bloody water covered me. They put me on a horse, and we started from there without breakfast. This was the fourth day without food. The water I drank the day before increased my fever, and I was so dry I could not expectorate.

We had then come to the Llano Estacado, so the country was open, but not exactly a desert. We traveled three or four hours, when all at once Pinero stopped and pointed down into the grass. I saw something with keen little eyes. The Indian made signs for me to get down and catch them, but I was afraid, as I knew not what they were. He jumped down and gathered them in his arms. They were little antelope, and we carried them away with us, two of them. After going some distance we stopped and built a big fire, arranged sticks and

CHAPTER IV

threw on these little antelope alive, hair, guts and all. We were hungry and had no time for niceties or butchering. That was the first eating we had enjoyed for four days, and we ravenously pulled the hair and picked the bones of those pretty little animals.

There is a peculiarity about these animals, the antelope. They seem to be between the goat and the deer. They sometimes leave their young for hours at a time hidden in the grass, but if anything disturbs them the mother is inquisitive enough to follow to see what becomes of her young, so we watched our back trail and soon had two older antelope for supper. We camped that night when the shades of darkness began to descend, but I was not treated so cruelly as on the night previous. I was only corded, and not weighted down.

CHAPTER V

WE REACH THE VILLAGE

After we cleaned up the antelope we traveled two days without food. We came in sight of a large woolly animal which I was sure would weigh a ton. He was very bulky, but he was fleet, and when both of the Indians charged him he ran for quite a distance. This was the first buffalo I ever saw, although I had heard my father speak of them. The animal had short, slightly curved horns, and a large hump on his back. Pinero and Chiwat soon killed him, cut him open, took out the entrails, and ate the food they found in his stomach, and the lining of his stomach. Then they cut off a piece of the liver and smeared gall over it and gave it to me to eat. I swallowed it, but it came back. I swallowed it down again, and again it came back. The Indians put more gall on it, and I held it down.

From there on we found game in abundance, and I learned to eat what was given me without vomiting. We traveled for at least ten days, and one day came upon a little knoll. Chiwat raised a red blanket and waved it a half circle and returned it the same way. The process was repeated several times. I watched the countenances of my companions, and at first they seemed to be perplexed,

17

but soon their faces brightened, and a smile broadened into a grin. They seemed to have forgotten me entirely; several keen yells escaped their lips, and they began urging their horses forward into a sweeping gallop. We soon came to an Indian village, which was located somewhere near the line of New Mexico, by a beautiful lake of water.

Yells, whoops and various sounds greeted our ears, as the Indians swarmed to meet us. This village must have contained 2,500 savages. Chiwat jumped off and left me, while Pinero led my horse on to Carnoviste's tent and halted. The squaws and children were yelling, hooting and making so much confusion I didn't know anything, and was badly frightened. Several of them rushed toward me and I thought my time had come. One fat, squabby, heathenish, hellish wench grabbed me, pulled me from the horse, pinched me, slapped me, beat me, threw me down, wallowed me, while the others looked on in great glee. At last the old profligate let me up, and the whole camp came marching around me, dancing and yelling. The old squaws were in the front group, the braves in the second squad, and the young girls and boys brought up the rear. The women chanted their incantations, the warriors fired their guns and yelled, and they had a great jubilee. This storm passed over, and out came an old buck with a big knife and caught me by the hair. I thought he was scalping me, but he was only shingling my hair. Of course he occasionally cut out a plug of the scalp and the blood trickled down my back, over my face, and covered my shoulders, but I kept a stolid countenance and tried to conceal my fright. Another of the pesky barbarians, who had been heating a small iron, came up and stuck that hot rod through my ear, burning a hole as it went, while others held me. He took the iron out and inserted a buckskin string through the hole he had made. He then repeated the process in the other ear. And then, seeming determined to add to my misery he turned the hot iron rod to my arms and burned great holes there. I have the scars yet to show as proof of these assertions. I fought, kicked and raved, but they beat and burned me until I could stand it no longer and I became exhausted. I wanted to die. I was poor, weak and faint, and I grew very sick; everything went dark, and I fell down and lay still. How long I lay there I do not know, but after they had punished me to their savage soul's desire, they took me up and were washing me when consciousness returned.

CHAPTER VI

I BECOME AN INDIAN

As in the eastern sky the curtain of night, with its mists of darkness, gloom and fears, rolls away and gives place to the glories of the coming day which flashes across the firmament in quivering lances of changing shades of vivid coloring, until lifted up and wakened into new life; the finer sensibilities of our nature are attuned in such harmony with the scene that they seem like chords of some magic music harp vibrating with the beauties which environ us, and which give promise of the coming day. Not so with me. I turned over on the hard ground, but I had been washed, bathed and oiled, and in many respects felt better, but I little knew what the future had in store for me. Pinero came and carried me to where the food was spread for a feast. Other warriors had at some previous time bartered with Mexicans and a blanket spread on the ground was supplied with sun-baked bread, peloncia, and cooked and raw meat was before me. Either on account of my extreme hunger or divine providence, I seized the raw meat and began to eat. That pleased the Indians and they immediately began to pat me. Had I first touched the cooked food—the bread, peloncia, and roasted meat, the food of civilized man, I would likely have been tortured to death. The Indians laughed, cut many capers, and made many signs so that I understood that I had pleased them. After the feast the Indians gave me a large jug and sent me to a lake nearby for water. This jug was made of dogwood, plaited or woven together, and cemented with pine pitch. It was strapped about my neck and I was sent into the lake to fill it. Several little Indian boys went with me. They showed me how to fill the jug by stooping down and allowing the water to flow in at the mouth of the jug until it was full, and then they helped me up, but the water was so heavy and I was so small and weak that it pulled me over and I fell, getting a ducking. When I tried to rise up again the water jug held me down. The boys laughed and assisted me to rise again, but just as I was straight they turned me loose and the jug pulled me over. Several times in succession I was ducked and became so strangled that I could not stand without the jug. Chiwat came and carried out the water and led me back to camp. I then laid down and rested for about three hours.

I was aroused, painted and made to wrestle and fight a while with the boys. They would get me down, but I would scratch, bite, kick and knock until I got on top. Then we would have another fall. Such was our camp life, from day to day. Precious time was wasted here. With those savages I was doomed to stay and grow up a heathen. I was deprived of schooling, the tender care of a father, and the fond love of a mother. On this occasion, after wrestling, fighting and racing until we were totally exhausted, we were washed, greased and painted. A squaw made me a buckskin jacket, moccasins and a cap.

When food became scarce we were sent down a little creek that had almost dried up, only stagnant pools remaining, and caught fish. I was so hungry that I wanted to eat the fish, but my companions told me that would offend the Great Spirit. I tried to argue the question, when the chief came up and getting the meaning of my talk he picked me up and tossed me over into the creek, probably with the invitation for me to help myself to the forbidden game. While in the mud I found a hard shelled turtle; the Indian boys were delighted with that, and soon joined me in catching turtles. When we had secured about fifty of these we took them to camp, where the squaws built up a big fire and threw them on the hot coals. Some would crawl out, only to be picked up and thrown back into the fire. They were roasted, shell, entrails and all, and we ate them and they were good.

CHAPTER VII

ATTEMPT TO ESCAPE

I was entrusted with a herd of horses, and shown the way to water, quite a long distance from camp. I was left by myself with the horses away out on the lonely prairie. When I looked away to the east over the blue mountains I would think of my situation and tears would flow. While my physical being, although somewhat scabby from recent sores, was comparatively at ease, yet there was a choking emotion, "an inward inexpressibility and an outward all-over-ness" which I had never felt before. Did you ever have this feeling? Civilized people call it homesickness. I would sit there on my pony and cry. I never cried while I was being tortured, nor when I ran the gauntlet, nor when I nearly drowned; in those times I gave a yell of defiance or a snarl of vengeance. But now in my loneliness and desolation I could weep. A new thought struck me, and my tears vanished, a smile flitted over my face. I made up my mind to escape. I carefully concealed what provisions I had in a buffalo robe, strapped a jug of water to my pony's neck, carefully surveyed the surrounding country, and mounted the pony allotted to me, and started east in a sweeping gallop. Had I viewed

23

the western horizon I would have seen a cloud of dust rising and known that my captors were giving chase. I did just what they expected me to do— make an effort to escape. I rode manfully for a boy of my age, but soon the pony stumbled and fell and I struck heavily on the ground, and hope and breath deserted me. It was only a matter of a few moments until I was overtaken, severely whipped with a rope, tightly bound, and carried back to camp. The Indians gathered around me, held a long council, whipped me again, and left me bound for some time.

After this a boy accompanied me and kept me from being so lonesome. He taught me their language, showed me how to fix arrows and make bows. We herded the horses and I waited on my master, Carnoviste, the chief; he stole me, so I belonged to him. I would get his horse, bring his food, light his pipe, bathe his feet, paint his skin, tighten the spikes on his arrows, catch lice on his head and body, and attend to what other chores he required, some not decent to put in this book.

I worked hard, and when I was not watching the herd, or administering to my master's needs, every old squaw had me trotting to her whims and fancies. I had to pound up the corn, skin the game, rub for fire, carry water, dress wounds and do many other things. Life became a burden to me, and once more I longed for death as relief. But to me no ray of hope could come. My fate was sealed; my doom was done.

After serving the vilest of the base for a while my situation was somewhat modified. I was permitted to associate more with the boys and girls of the village. Carnoviste began to teach me to ride wild horses, to jump from the ground astraddle the horse as he ran by, and dodge an arrow at the same time. I was taught to crouch closely to the neck of the horse so an enemy could not hit me, and how to use the shield and ward off arrows. I have often been asked how the Indians made their shields, and I will here try to tell. To make a shield required several days time. The Indian took the hide of an old bull (sometimes the thick part of the buffalo hide was used), cut a round piece from the neck and shoulders, threw this over the fire and heated it while green. When it was as hot as it would stand without burning it was then rubbed on a rough rock until the meat was erased, then a smooth stone was used until the hide became very smooth, soft and pliable. A rattan or hickory withe was made into a hoop, and the rawhide was strapped on and sewed with thongs of rawhide, and then it was given the necessary "dish" by stretching over stakes, and left to dry. After the shield is thoroughly dry and cured it is set up as a target, and if an arrow pierces it or a bullet goes through it, it finds a place among the debris of the camp, but if it proves war-proof it occupies a place with the warriors and a strong string is placed through each side so it can be held on the arm. The hairy side is next to the arm and the slick side facing the enemy. The moon, stars, serpents, turtles and other designs are painted on the shield and in such location that they serve as a compass to guide and direct the Indian owner on a cloudy day.

I was given a shield and placed off about fifty yards. Four braves took bows and blunt arrows and began to shoot at me. I knew what I had to do, for I had seen the performance before. I began moving the shield up and down and from right to left. The arrows poured against it and I managed to ward them off with the wavy motion, but torrents of blunt sticks came and I was too slow. One passed just over the shield and struck me in the forehead. I saw stars—not those painted ones on my shield, but real fiery flashes—it downed me and those comrades let up the shooting for a time, but the target practice was soon resumed, and I had to learn how to use the shield. I was knocked down several times before I became an adept. All Indians were thus trained.

After this they taught me how to ride races. I was tied on the horse the way I was expected to sit, nearly straight, leaning a little forward, with my knees clamping the horse so as to cut the wind. After they quit tying me I fell off several times. The horse would sometimes fly the track and would have to be run down on the prairie, with me swinging under his belly when I was tied on. In training we would run around a lake, but in the gambling a straight track was used, so neither horse would have the advantage.

All Indians tried their luck in games of chance. They had a game called "plava-penyole," which was played with five sticks painted red on one side and blue on the other. The fifth stick had a red cross on it. They would cast them up like dice; all one color up was the highest, and the cross was the "king." They would bet on these sticks, foot races, horse races, or anything that came along. Sometimes luck would go against a brave and he would lose all of his worldly possessions, including his wife and children.

The Apaches were mean to their squaws, and indulgent to their children. At the age of twelve boys were taught to pilfer, rob and steal.

CHAPTER VIII

NARROW ESCAPE OF MY PEOPLE

It was the custom of the Indians that when an Indian captured a white child, that child became the property of that particular Indian. Therefore, according to tribal custom, I belonged to Carnoviste, and was called his son. He gave me an Indian name, En Da, meaning "white boy." His squaw, Laughing Eyes, was very good to me and treated me as her own. At that time she had no child of her own, and she lavished affection upon me, and in my childish way I returned her caresses. Later when her baby, Straight Bow, was born she did not cease to bestow motherly affection upon me, and when she died a year later I felt that I had lost my best friend among the Indians.

After I had been with the Indians about two months, Carnoviste and eleven of his braves started on another raid down into the settlements where the white people lived, and they visited that region where I was captured. When they returned they brought back a drove of stolen horses, and Carnoviste and another Indian, named Genava, were carrying gunshot wounds, which had been inflicted by my own mother when they attacked her home. The Indians gave me an account of the attack and told me they had killed my mother and all of my people, and showed me clothing and a small pistol which I recognized as my own. They beat me unmercifully, and I am sure if either Carnoviste or Genàva had died of their wounds I would certainly have been put to death. My mother had used a shotgun loaded with No. 4 turkey shot, which had peppered the breast of Carnoviste, while Genava caught a full charge at the lower end of his back, which forced him to either lie on his stomach or stand up. He could not sit down. For a long time it was thought he would die. The process of picking shot from these rascals occupied much time, and was generally accompanied by grunts and howls of pain. As to a full account of this attack on my mother's home, I had only the Indians' version of it, but years afterward, when I was restored to my people I learned the truth, and I will let my sister, Mina, now Mrs. John Keyser, tell it just as it happened, and in her own way:

"In 1870, two months after Herman was stolen, my step-father, Philip Buchmier, and my brother, Adolph Lehmann, were about a mile from home irrigating land. My other brother, Willie Lehmann, and I drove the horses to water. On the west side of the creek was a high bluff and while the horses were drinking a big rock rolled down the bluff and struck near me. I told Willie that we must run home; that it might be Indians. We waded into the water and drove the horses out. Not having enough water they went reluctantly, but we hurried them to the pasture and then ran to the house. Mother had to do all of the sewing for her large family by hand in those days, so she put me to sewing up the long straight seams. We had not been sitting there long until the dog began to bark. I looked out to see what he was barking at but could see nothing. In a few minutes he set up barking again, and we thought father was coming home with the cows and calves, and as he always scolded if the gate was not opened, I rushed out toward the gate, and to my horror, there came twelve big Indian warriors in a gallop, holding their shields before them, moving to and fro like snakes, their long hair dangling in the air. How hideous and frightful they looked! They did not yell or make any more noise than was necessary. Silence is a characteristic trait of the Apache, while the Comanche always shouted, yelled and made all the noise possible. They rode around the house, about fifty yards away, the first round, but kept circling, coming a little nearer each time. I fetched in the axe and we closed and barred the doors. The smaller children were terribly frightened and mother was somewhat nervous from excitement, seeing that we had to contend against such fearful odds, but we silently sent up our petitions to the Great Providence. At first I trembled and a sense of fainting came over me, but all this soon passed off and I felt bold and determined—even furious. By this time the Indians had closed in on us and began throwing rocks and sticks through the windows. I pushed the children under the bed, but they kept trying to crawl out. When the Indians first surrounded the house mother wanted to shoot, but I advised her not to do so until they attempted to enter the room. Finally the chief ventured to appear in the window. I held the gun up and mother took aim and pulled the trigger, and the Indian dropped. The full charge struck his shield, and glanced into his addomen. Several other Indians approached and we fired our second shot, again striking a shield, but this time the shot scattered, wounding two or three. I forgot to tell you they had captured all of the horses. At first they fired about twenty shots with their short guns. As they came closer to the house mother looked out through the window, and whizz! came a lance, passing close to her temple and stuck in the table nearby. After a few more charges, in which they were careful not to expose themselves

CHAPTER VIII

to the shotgun fire, they gave up the siege and galloped away. When father and Adolph came they
became so enraged they wanted to follow them,
but we persuaded them not to go. When the Indians disappeared and we opened the door, there
stood our faithful old dog, Max. Several lance
wounds and the torn-up turf in the yard showed
that the brave old dog had done his part, but his
honest eyes looked pleadingly into those of his mis-
tress and then he fell over exhausted from loss of
blood. Part of the time during the fight I stood
by one of the windows with a long cane knife while
mother guarded the other with an axe. Some Indians went into the other room, took all the blankets, broke up the furniture, cut open the feather
beds, and wrecked things generally. The Indian
that mother shot was the very villain who stole
Herman."

My other sister, Mrs. Caroline Dye, now of Dallas,
in speaking of this attack, said there was a large
goods box on the front porch, in which were some
articles of clothing. The Indians emptied this box,
and found a small pistol, which they showed me
when they returned, and which I recognized as my
own property. Naturally, I believed their yarn
when they told me they had killed all of my people.

32

CHAPTER IX

I GO ON A RAID

The Indians were cowards, and whenever there was danger they would send me. The first raid I accompanied them on they stole a bunch of horses near the head of the San Saba River, and in the herd were two large sorrel mules. The first I tried to steal was a large black horse staked near Fort Concho. The Indians were afraid to go up to him, for they thought somebody was watching. Carnoviste told me to go for the horse. I hesitated. He drew his gun on me and commanded me to go, and of course I consented—a boy can't answer such argument. He gave me a pistol and I moved cautiously toward the horse, crawling part of the way. I saw something bulky near the horse and thought I could see it move. I was within three feet of the bulk. I cut the rope that held the horse, when suddenly the man (for it was a man) rose up and shot at me, the charge passing just over my head, but the smoke and fire blinded my eyes and the noise made me deaf in one ear for a month. I was so excited that I dropped my pistol and forgot to get it in my haste to get away from there. The noise and confusion stampeded the horse, and I think the man must have run, too. I ran a short distance and hid in the high grass and lay still for a long time. After a while I heard wolves howling and went to them, not wolves, but my companions, for that was our signal when we were separated. I told the Indians that the pistol was shot out of my hand, and that it fell in reach of the white man. Had I told the truth I would have had to have gone back for the precious weapon.

We came down the San Saba to about Voca and then turned south, crossed Mason county and slept a while near Hedwig's Hill, on the Llano River. We went down the river to near the town of Llano. Near Llano we rushed up on some men who had stopped and stacked their arms for dinner. We put them to flight, destroyed their camp, stole their horses and went on our way rejoicing, but we changed our course and made for House Mountain, so we could survey the country and see if we were followed. We killed a fat beef and roasted him on top of the mountain, had a feast and rest there, and then went up Hickory. We saw two white men coming toward us. We sat still until they were within 100 yards of us and then we showed ourselves. One man rode away, but the other stayed long enough to send up his compliments with two bullets, and then he, too, turned to run. We charged, but our man was not much of a coward, for occasionally he returned a shot. We crowded them so close they quit their horses and hid in a thicket, and we drove off their horses.

We came back near my old home, and somewhere near Beaver Creek we stole more horses. By that time we had a good herd, but the scouts came in and reported a band of white men following us. On Little Devil's River we were overtaken and several shots were exchanged at long range. None of our party was injured, so we changed our course and went northwest, and away up on the head of Bear Creek the whites overtook us again, and this time the fight was at close range. One Indian was severely wounded, but afterwards recovered. We made our get-away from there, and nothing else eventful happened until we reached our village, where we found signs which told the warriors why the village had been deserted, and which direction the squaws and children had gone. Another Indian tribe had driven them northward. The chief easily followed their trail, although I could see no signs. We still had our horses and reached camp all right.

We hunted on the plains a while and came back south. In the summer time we wore nothing but a breech-clout. The warriors found a bee-cave on the side of a bluff which must have been fully 200 feet high. From all indications there was an abun-

CHAPTER IX

dance of honey in the cave, but how to get it—that was the question. We had a hide sewed up and lined with the paunch of an old bull; it would hold several gallons. We had a good supply of ropes. We went around and climbed up on top of the bluff from the other side and came up over the cave. A consultation was held and they decided to send me down. Ropes were tied together until they would reach the cave below. A stout stick was fastened to the end of this strong rope, and after tying the bag onto the rope and around my waist also, I was put astraddle the rope on that stick and lowered down the bluff. I would strike the bank and push myself away from sharp projecting rocks. Down, down, I descended until I came even with the bee-cave and there I was stopped. This was a cloudy, damp day and the bees were out of humor, but I went naked in among them, filled my bag with nice new honey and comb, and hooted to be drawn up. This performance was repeated several times, and in this way we secured enough honey to last for a long time. There was plenty of honey left in the cave for the bees, too. Far back in the cave could be seen great clusters of comb honey, much of it black with age, and the storage must have been going on for years. This cave reminds me of the bee cave on Squaw Creek near Hedwig's Hill, which I have seen in recent years, and which has never been robbed. It is situated high up on a bluff overhanging the river. Below it is a deep lake of water, and it sometimes happens that the honey is seen running down the face of the cliff to the water below. I have been told that the bees have never swarmed from this cave, and old settlers say they have known of its existence for over sixty years.

CHAPTER X

ON A RAID

From our village we started on a raid upon the white settlements, to get more horses, and to kill as many of the palefaces as we could. The Apaches never carried their squaws or children along on a thieving raid, while the Comanches did. One of the braves, Tusciwhoski (Whitewood), and his squaw had fallen out. He had caught her in adultery with a Mexican trader. He killed the trader, and cut off his wife's nose, which was the penalty of a squaw for such offenses, and when we started on the raid he said: "I will never come back; I am going to die." We knew he would make good his boast, even if he had to take his own life. We traveled on, and rode for miles without Tusciwhoski saying a word. When we came in sight of Kickapoo Springs we discovered a white man, nicely dressed. Tusciwhoski said, "I will get that man." It was the Indian custom to turn the painted side of the shield out, but he had the fur side out, and when the chief called his attention to it and said the Great Spirit would not assist a warrior who would be so unreverential, Tusciwhoski said, "The white man and I must both die." And thus saying, he dashed toward the white man, who was about

38

HERMAN LEHMANN IN COMANCHE WAR BONNET

three hundred yards away. Silence reigned supreme, while we watched the maneuvers of our companion. He dashed up to the white man and fired his Winchester, and the white man returned the salute with a 44-calibre Colt's revolver. Several shots were exchanged while the white man beat a slow and dogged retreat. We saw our companion reel and fall to the ground, and hurried to him, but he was dead. We hastened toward the white man, but he, too, tumbled from his horse and made an effort to rise, but failed. He made several attempts to shoot us, but was too far gone. He rolled over on his face and expired. We examined him closely and found four bullet holes in his breast made by Winchester balls. We did not scalp or otherwise disfigure this man, because he was brave and fearless. He was riding a large gray horse, had a fine silver mounted Mexican saddle, new red blanket, a stout heavy bridle, with shop-made bits, and in his saddle pockets we found a great quantity of silver and a roll of greenbacks. The bills we tore up, not knowing anything about their value. We took the sixshooter and other things and went back to the dead Indian. In his breast we found three holes where pistol balls had entered and in his back three torn places where the bullets had come out. These balls readily passed through the hairy side of

CHAPTER X

the shield. We buried Tusciwhoski in a little cave, after wrapping his body in buffalo robes and placing his weapons by his side. His horse we killed and left near him. There we left one of the bravest and best of the Apache tribe.

We went down about Fort Territt and found some Rangers camped there. Their horses were loose, scattered around. We rounded up thirty or more and drove them away. Some were hobbled with chains and locked, and we could not get these irons off, so we cut off the horses' feet to keep the Rangers from using them any more. If we could not have them, the Rangers could not. One fine gray horse we carried along in hopes of being able to get his hobbles off by breaking the lock, but he, too, had to share the fate of the others.

We came into a plain road and discovered a wagon in which there was a man and woman and three children. Before they were aware of our presence we had them surrounded, and it was but the work of a few seconds to kill and scalp the man, woman and a little baby; the two other children we carried with us, a little girl about eight, and a boy about six years old. The man was working an ox team. We killed the oxen and burned the wagon with its dead occupants. We went north, and just as we were crossing a little ravine

40

four white men dashed in between us and our herd of horses. This was so sudden and so daring we were for a moment thrown into confusion. We rallied and turned on them, soon putting them to flight. One of the white men lost his pistol, and Carnoviste got it. The whites outran us, driving our horses before them, but we held on to the captive children. The poor little things would not eat. We carried them four days and nights and they cried all of the time. We could not slip up and steal anything for the noise they made, so two big buck Indians rode up, one on each side of the little girl. The one on the left took her left hand and foot, and the Indian on the right side took her right hand and foot. They raised her from the horse on which she sat and drove the horse away and swung her three times, the third time turning her loose. She cut a somersault in the air, and when she struck the ground she was dead, and every Indian rode over the mangled corpse. The boy was served the same way at the same time by two other warriors. The bruised and trampled bodies were picked up and hung on a little tree for the vultures.

I hesitate to recite these revolting crimes, but they were true instances of the savagery in which I was engulfed through no choice of my own, and

CHAPTER X

I tell of them in order to show the venomous hatred cherished by the Indian against the whites.

We traveled on and just north of Beaver Lake we came to a big clear hole of water. Here we killed a buffalo, built up a fire and roasted some of the ribs. Some of the Indians were in bathing, when suddenly the Rangers charged upon us. At the first fire two of our braves fell. We grabbed our weapons and went into a chaparral near by, and the Rangers got all of our horses and everything else except what we could pick up as we rushed away. We were pretty well scattered as we made our way from there, and we did not all get back to our village, which we reached, one, two, three and five together. Three more of our band were killed and one severely wounded, but he made his way to camp. When we brought in the news of our bad luck there was great mourning. Such hideous cries, such mournful howls! The squaws cut themselves all to pieces with knives. The squaw of the wounded warrior burned her own arm every morning that she might not forget her grief until her master's wound should heal. For several days straggling warriors came in, and the camp was a spectacle of grief, sorrow and despair. To add to the desolation of the scene, another defeated party came in carrying one wounded and reported one killed. A third party, who had gone on a raid, returned defeated, four dead and one taken captive. I learn he was brought down the old trail to San Antonio by the soldiers. We were sure we had offended the Great Spirit, so our medicine man began his incantations and howlings, went up on a hill and waved cows' tails, and we all fasted. Then a fourth raiding party came in with horses and scalps, and a better humor prevailed in camp.

Some time after this we were stopping at a beautiful water place when a party of Comanches visited us, and among them was a German boy named Adolph Korn, who was captured by the Comanches in Mason County a short time after my capture. We talked over our situation. We could both speak German, so our Indian masters did not understand us. We had a good time and would have devised some means of escape had we not been disturbed; but the Comanches left, taking Korn with them, and I had to go back to my old associates and catch lice for Carnoviste.

CHAPTER XI

I SCALP A MEXICAN

On a raid twelve of us made, on our way down to the settlements, we came upon four buffalo hunters. I think they were Mexicans and white men together. We had camped on a creek and had killed a big fat buffalo bull and had a big feast. One of our warriors was stationed on a high point to watch for Rangers, and when another went to relieve him, they discovered the four buffalo hunters coming towards us on foot, their camp being behind a hill some distance away. The alarm was given, and all of us went to watch these buffalo hunters to see if they were trailing us or what they were up to. We soon became convinced that they were not aware of our presence, so we made a charge on them, running our horses toward them as fast as we could go. When we were within a short distance of them they saw us and turned and ran, three of them going up on a hill where they got behind some rocks, the other man running toward camp. Seeing that the three men who had gone up on the hill and taken refuge behind the rocks were well fortified and bent upon putting up a stiff fight, we turned our attention to the man who was headed for camp, and we overtook him

44

in an open place. When we came near he began
to talk to us in Spanish. He told the Indians there
was nobody at the camp. The Indians left me in
charge of the Mexican and told me not to let him
get away while they went to rob the camp. Soon
I heard firing in the direction of the camp, and it
developed that the Mexican had told us a big lie,
for when the Indians arrived at the camp there
were several men in the camp and they opened fire
on the Indians. When the Mexican heard the shooting he began picking up rocks and throwing them
at me. I took a shot at him with my bow, but
the arrow barely grazed him. He then threw up
his hands in token of complete surrender, and I
kept him covered until the Indians returned. As
the men in camp were making it pretty hot for the
Indians, they retreated and came back over the
hill to where I and the Mexican were, and when I
told Carnoviste about the Mexican throwing rocks
at me, he became enraged and ordered me to kill
him at once. I shot him through the heart with
an arrow and he fell dead. Not satisfied with forc-
ing me to kill this Mexican, Carnoviste ordered me
to take his scalp, but I did not want to do it, for
I had never before scalped anybody and I did not
relish the task, but my chief threatened me with all
kinds of punishment if I did not do as he ordered,

so I took my knife, made an incision all around the top of his head, grasped his hair with my fingers and gave a quick jerk backwards and the scalp came off with a report like a pop-gun.

The Indians gathered around and made me turn the body face downward. Carnoviste then told me to cut a cross on an arrow and lay it on the dead man's back, which I did. While doing so the Indians smoked a pipe, blew the smoke on their breasts, and held their hands toward the sun, palms outward, in some kind of worship, beseeching the Great Spirit to let good fortune attend them and give them victory over all enemies. Why the cross was cut on that arrow I cannot say, unless it was to mark it as a weapon which had shed human blood. An Indian never used an arrow the second time which had killed a man, enemy or friend. It was stained with human blood.

We mounted our horses and left there, leaving those buffalo hunters safely fortified among the rocks on the hill and in their camp. We proceeded on to the settlements, where we stole a large number of horses and made our return trip safely.

CHAPTER XII

BATTLE WITH COMANCHES

Bobo, a young Indian, and I went hunting one morning, bright and early. I was on a dun mule which had been beaten over the head a great deal, and was subject to the "studs" (balkiness). Whenever I wanted him to run he would stop and whirl around and around. At that time we were at war with the Comanches. We had gone some distance from the camp when we saw, coming over the hill, a big band of Comanches in full war paint. Bobo was riding a swift pony, so he ran off and left me, although I yelled loudly, "Toko! toko!" (wait! wait). The arrows came whizzing about, and I heard one go zip! and a small spike embedded itself in that old mule's hip. He was no longer a permanent fixture on the landscape, but suddenly developed into a moving, progressive hybrid that gained speed as he moved. I had no trouble whatever with the locomotion of that mule. My main thought was to ride. The whizz of the arrows was soon lost but I could hear the war-whoop of the forty infuriated warriors on my track. I was too near out of breath to look back, so I hugged my mule and leaned over in order not to accumulate too much wind, and rode like a race rider. I passed Bobo, and heard his entreaty not to leave him, nor depart from following after him, but if I had any intention of waiting it was forlorn, for that dun mule was on the go. There was no stopping or holding him. He passed through camp at a furious rate, knocking down squaws and children, and demoralizing things in general. He continued on beyond the camp to the horse herd, and there he checked his fast career and began kicking and bucking for dear life. I quit him then and caught a pony and hastened back to camp, and got there in time to be in the desperate battle which had begun. Bobo was overtaken and scalped near the village, and the Apaches had forced the Comanches back and surrounded his body. Every foot of ground was contested. The Comanches were nasty fighters, but we greatly outnumbered them. The battle began about 10 o'clock in the morning and raged most of the day. About sundown the Comanches withdrew, leaving many of their comrades dead on the battlefield. We never tried to follow them, for twenty of our braves had gone to the happy hunting grounds, while eight more were writhing in pain, four of whom died that night in spite of the prayers and incantations of our medicine man; one more died the next day, but the other three recovered. Our dead were given decent burial. We went over the ground held by the Comanches and took possession of all the guns, bows and arrows, shields, and what horses that were not dead or wounded. We gathered up the Comanche carcasses and threw them in a hole in the ground and left them uncovered.

We then moved our village further north. Soon two Comanche spies were discovered; one was ambushed and killed, and the other captured and retained for a worse fate. Carnoviste cut a hole through each of his arms, drew a rawhide cord through the openings and hung the poor fellow up in a mesquite tree to die, but an unfaithful old squaw, without a nose, slipped back and cut him down.

We moved on about sixty miles to a spring, and prepared to camp there permanently, or for a few months at least. We had been there several days and had grown a bit careless when one night one of the Indians dreamed that a large band of Comanches were after us and that we would be overpowered and suffer great losses. The next morning a great council was held and a difference of opinion prevailed. We had speaking and fasting all day. The majority were in favor of getting out of the way of the Comanches, so we started on the move again, and had gone about twenty miles when we found ourselves surrounded by the enemy. Our women and children were captured, forty warriors were killed, many were wounded, our horses were driven away, our camp equipment was taken and we were in destitute and desperate straits. I do not know about the losses of the Comanches, but we had rifles, which did very effective firing, and I am sure many were killed. Something like one hundred warriors, six women and myself made our escape on foot. We turned back and drifted around for about a month, generally going in a southern direction. We met one hundred and fifty Apaches well mounted and equipped with surplus arms and horses. They supplied our needs and we all moved on south together, a little happier than we had been for a month.

We sent out scouts in all directions and called for the scattering bands of the Apache tribe to come together at a certain lake on the plains. Time was allowed for the members of the tribe who were in Arizona, Utah, and Mexico to come together. In the meantime we were making bows and arrows, and gathering all of the guns, ammunition and war equipment we could accumulate. Weapons were being manufactured in every wigwam, ponies were trained, squaws and children were given instruction, and we were getting ready for war.

Victorio, the big chief, and his favorite scouts

went out to look for the Comanches. In about
three moons warriors began to come in from every
source, and thousands were ready to help us rescue
our women and children. In a few days, before
our forces were fully recruited, Victorio returned
alone. He and his scouts had had a fight with the
Comanches, and all were killed except Victorio; he
was too smart to be caught.

Victorio, Geronimo and other chiefs made
speeches. Victorio favored peace. He said, "I
fear not the Comanches myself, neither am I afraid
of their allies, the Kiowas; but these tribes are
strong among themselves and greatly outnumber
us. Besides, the whites furnish them with guns
and powder and lead, to help exterminate our tribe.
The white man is the Indian's enemy, and the Indians must quit fighting among themselves and all
go together to fight the palefaces. While I was
gone I saw as many palefaces as there are sprigs
of grass on the plains or stars in the sky, and if
we continue to fight each other we will all be exterminated by the white men."

Red Wasp said: "We do not fear the cowardly
palefaces. They have robbed us of our hunting
grounds, they have destroyed our game, they have
brought us disease, they have stirred up discord
among our own race, they intimidated our braves,

they have made profligates of our children, repro-
bates. of our wives and destroyed our traditions.
They have wrought despair and desolation to our
tribe, and for my part I am ready to fight until I
fall. As to the Comanches, our grievances are
great and the cause of the war is just, and I'll be
glad to kill them when they come, kill them as
they kill our companions, kill them, kill them. And
if we must die, let us fight to the bitter end. I want
to fight."

Other speeches followed pro and con, but the
opinion prevailed that all Indians should unite in
one great effort to exterminate the palefaces, and
for the common cause emissaries were sent to the
several tribes, with the result that a treaty was
finally consummated which resulted in the return
of our women and children.

We moved toward the Comanches and camped
within three miles of their village and raised a flag
of truce. The Comanches sent out a warrior, who
galloped around us at a safe distance, waving a
black shield in the air, which meant fight, death
to the vanquished, and had the Apaches sent a man
in return with a red shield it would have meant we
accept the challenge and are ready to fight, but we
raised a white flag and that meant peace. The Comanches made signs that six of their men would

meet an equal number of our men on half-way ground. The warriors were collected and ready for battle at the slightest signal. The Comanches agreed to make peace if we would deliver to them the men who split open the Comanche's arms and hanged him up in the tree, but we promptly disavowed the act and declared that the warriors who did it had been killed in battle, but one of the very men who formed our commission was one of the guilty parties. So the Comanches, trusting to our honor and veracity, agreed to the treaty and our women and children were returned, all except the woman who cut down the Comanche. She was adopted by the Comanches, for we did not want her, for she had had her nose cut off for unfaithfulness to her husband. Some of the maidens had been chosen by the Comanches and these were allowed to stay, and thus the tie of union was more securely bound.

To Victorio belongs the credit of this treaty, and some of his daring experiences would not be out of place here. Once he was out hunting and killed a buffalo. The weather was intensely cold. He dressed the buffalo and night overtook him. He had no other covering except the warm hide of the buffalo, so he enveloped himself in the hide. The night waned, and the morning came, but the norther was still here. Victorio attempted to rise, but to his horror he was tightly bound. The raw buffalo hide was stiffly frozen and Victoria was unable to move hand or foot. He was thus imprisoned for two days and nights, but the third day the sun shone out and the Indian managed to get free. Another time, in Mexico, we were fighting the Mexican soldiers when one of Victorio's brothers was captured. (I was up on a hill watching the conflict.) Victorio rode down a canyon, and under the cover of the smoke, he rode in among the soldiers waving his shield, and his brother, who was a prisoner of the Mexicans, jumped up behind him and they rode back to our men amid the cross-fire of the battle, but just as they reached our line a ball struck Victorio's brother in the back, passed through his body, went into Victorio's back and came out at his breast. The brother fell off the horse dead. Victorio turned and saw that his brother was past all earthly aid; he dismounted, placed the dead Indian on his horse, leaped up behind and rode on to our headquarters. When he reached there he was covered with blood, and presented a horrible sight. He was given immediate attention, the wound was probed and the bruised part was cut away, and treated with a solution made from some kind of a weed and clear water, and

Victorio finally recovered, although the ball must have passed through his right lung.

Victorio was a remarkable Indian, and gave the white people lots of trouble, as well as the Mexicans. He did many daring deeds, and the Mexican government offered a reward of $1,500 for his scalp. He had four wives and several good-looking daughters, and one time he offered to trade me a real pretty girl for a saddle I had captured, but I declined. Once in Mexico a warrior was captured and forced to tell where Victorio was. He was located under a bluff, well armed and equipped. He killed every man who tried to approach, and at nightfall made his escape. Once he decoyed a party of hunters into the Black Hills, got them separated and killed the whole company. It was said that he stole more white children than any two divisions of the Apache tribe.

CHAPTER XIII

SOME ADVENTURES

Eventually we consummated a treaty with the Kiowas also, and all prepared to annoy the palefaces as much as possible and kill as many as we could. In order to do our work secretly and more effectively we divided into small squads or bands.

The band to which I belonged went down into the settlements around Fredericksburg and Mason. One night some of us went into Fredericksburg, and there we saw some men in a saloon drinking beer; we let them drink in peace, but we took charge of all the horses we could find. We then went up on the hill north of town and I went into a man's lot and got two good horses, and my companions captured a nice herd nearby. We went north, some traveling the road and others exploring the country on each side. We got several good mules from one of my old neighbors, Fritz Ellebracht, and somewhere the party captured a boy about thirteen years old. We passed right by my old home, and the Indians tried to get me to go to my people. They called me paleface and urged me to quit them. I looked at the old house, and saw it was vacant, no one living there, but I knew very well that if I stopped I would be killed on the spot.

We went on and stole some horses from William Bickenbach, and then hurried out of that section, reaching our encampment with about forty good horses and mules, several scalps and one captive. We kept that boy about a year, but as he would not take to our ways, we traded him to some Mexicans. Whether he ever succeeded in getting back to his people I do not know, nor do I remember who he was.

Next we went on a raid with a band of Kiowas across the Pecos. Met some cowboys and had a fight with them, killed two of them and the others escaped. We scalped the dead ones and left their carcasses for the buzzards. These cowboys had a good bunch of ponies which we "corraled" and drove off with us. One of our Kiowa comrades was wounded and later died.

We went back to camp and moved southeast. Some of the warriors went on a raid, but I stayed in camp. Carnoviste went along, and when he returned two white scalps dangled from his belt, and a little white boy was brought in. They claimed to have killed two whole families.

We changed our plans and went about 300 miles into the pines of New Mexico, and among the mountains we killed deer, bear and wild sheep.

Finally our chiefs made a treaty with the whites

and soldiers in uniform came into our camp. Another white boy and I were kept hidden in the forest. This other boy would not stay, but would slip back to camp when he thought it time for the white inspector to come, so Snapping Turtle carried him away out into a thicket and left him tied to a tree, without food or water, and there he died.

The soldiers kept close guard over the Indians for three moons and I had to stay in hiding in the woods, but I would slip up to the wigwam of my old chief and get food.

We stayed there for some time, when the soldiers quit coming around regularly, thinking no doubt we were pretty well in hand, but some of our boys stole some horses and ran away and we all broke out and followed. I may here state that our band did not comprise all of the Apache tribe, as there were several bands which had not made a treaty.

We roamed over our old haunts and enjoyed the freedom of the plains. We crossed the Pecos and were preparing for a raid into Mexico, when a pestilence broke out among us. A great many died and among them was Carnoviste's wife. They carried her to the burying ground and laid her to rest with her two favorite dogs and all of her other valuables and trinkets. Everything was killed that belonged to her, and I was led up to be slain also.

The bows were strung and all was in readiness, when suddenly a young Indian maiden rushed forward and threw her arms around me, and I was spared. Her embrace and entreaties saved my life. Carnoviste's squaw left a small baby and I had to take care of it. A kindly squaw nursed it for me.

Our people continued to die from the disease, and our medicine man seemed not to understand it, but one old Indian, a noted medicine man, went up on a high mountain and there he offered up his prayers to the Great Spirit to come to his aid in combating the pestilence. It was winter time, and despite the cold he spent the night on that mountain. The next morning when he returned to camp he commanded that a hole be dug near the river. When this was done, he ordered that big fires be made and large stones be heated. The stones were placed in an air-tight wigwam. The sick Indians were stripped and placed in the air-tight wigwam and sweated as long as they could stand it; then they were suddenly plunged into almost freezing water and kept there for several minutes, and when they were brought out the cold norther froze icicles on their hair. We then rubbed them with wet grass, and a rough blanket, wrapped them in warm buffalo robes and gave them a strong drink of hot, bitter tea. This tea was made from the root of a plant that is in-

CHAPTER XIII

digenous to this country, but I do not know the name of it. The sick ones were treated and the well ones had to undergo the same treatment, and then we moved our camp, the well ones carrying the sick ones. No more Indians died from that plague.

ECHICONI, APACHE

CHAPTER XIV

BACK TO THE RESERVATION

After recuperating from the effects of the pestilence which had swept our camp with such disastrous results, we moved north and came in sight of soldiers, but we changed our course and were unobserved by them. In a day or two they struck our trail, but we decoyed them to the plains, a route where there was no water. We made the trail plain. After several days they sent out scouts who found a spring, and there they camped. We watched them closely and tried to steal their horses, but we could never catch them off their guard. Finally they hoisted a white flag, and we did the same. They sent out a man and Indehe went out to meet him, but just before they came together Indehe discharged his Winchester at the white man and ran him back to his comrades. We struck out into Mexico. The soldiers followed us, but we crossed back into New Mexico and were driven back into the reservation, and there we gave up and promised not to run away any more. I always had to "keep hid," or be killed by the red men. I was afraid of the whites anyway.

Different parties of our tribe would sometimes

have their camps as much as fifteen miles apart. An old Indian brought me out a large quantity of beer. We both drank freely. He boasted of how he treated me when I was first captured and made fun of me for being a paleface. We were both tipsy. I drew my six-shooter and ran the impudent rascal away. I took after him, shooting as I ran, and when the last chamber was empty I tumbled into a ditch, and lay there until nearly sundown. I don't think I hit that Indian, but anyway I was trying to.

One day, when no soldiers were around our camp, an Indian and his squaw had a fight. The warrior got a good beating, and came out second best in the brawl. He crawled away and picked up an old cap-and-ball rifle and was just ready to shoot the squaw when I wrenched the gun from him, cocked it and removed the cap. Just as I was letting the hammer down it slipped and fell hard on the tube. The cap was an old "G-D" and left sulphur on the tube. The gun fired, just as an old squaw walked right in front of me with wood in her arms. She tumbled over, and I ran away. I thought I had killed her. Accidents are not excusable in Indian life. To kill an Indian means to be killed by the nearest relative of the deceased. I learned that night from my sweetheart that the ball had struck the wood and knocked the old woman down, and that she was not hurt, so I was at liberty to return to camp. I slept in Carnoviste's wigwam that night. The next morning I went to drive up the horses. I rode a gentle horse and had a rope around his neck and a half-hitch over his nose. I made a loop in the other end of the rope and threw it around the neck of another horse. My horse stopped, but the other horse began to pitch and rear. I jumped off, and horse No. 2 broke my horse's neck. Carnoviste beat me nearly to death for this.

Another party of our tribe came in and with them was a beautiful Mexican girl. The Indian to whom she belonged wanted us to marry, and to this proposition Carnoviste acquiesced, and made me a long argumentative talk to that effect. The price of the girl was two horses, and these Carnoviste offered to pay. I thought she was the prettiest girl I ever saw. They fastened us up together in the same wigwam. But she did not want a husband and I did not want a wife, and furthermore, I did not intend to have somebody select one for me. So a well arranged match did not materialize.

Some warriors bought little girls, six or seven years old, and trained them up according to their fancy.

CHAPTER XIV

While there on the Apache reservation in New Mexico, the White Pine Reservation, it often happened that the Indians would get whisky and mescal, and in their drunken carousals would fight among themselves, and many times would kill each other. One time a feud broke out in which my party of friends were pitted against another band of Apaches, and we killed all of them. Not caring to be tried for this by the reservation authorities (white men), we decided to sneak away, and accordingly about a hundred of us, including squaws, bucks and children, left one night and when morning came it found us many miles away. As we were traveling along we came upon a party of movers in camp. One man was watching the horses. He was sitting on a horse in order to see further away. He was thrown from his horse and Zunde, one of the Indians, rushed upon him. The paleface used his hat for a shield, whereupon the Indian shot and killed him. We then stampeded the horses and ran them off, not caring to attack the camp, for we discovered the men there were well armed and could put up a good fight.

We went on through to the plains and met another party of our tribe who had been for a long time in Mexico. A Mexican boy was along with whom I often fought, and he always whipped me.

BACK TO THE RESERVATION

He and I were placed on fast horses and made to run a horse race. My horse came out ahead, and my Indian won. He was bragging on me and said that I was the better rider. The Mexican's master said I might beat his boy riding, but Mexicano could whip me, and a wager was laid. I knew that if I didn't whip that Mexican that time I would get a terrible beating. We hitched. Mexicano was stouter than I, so he downed me and was giving me a sure enough flogging, when my arms stole up and my fingers became entangled in his long black hair. I gave a few jerks, made a quick twist of my body and found myself on top. I took new courage and did some hard pounding myself. We were cheered and hissed, and both arose and went to kicking each other. I got in a good lick below the belt and cut off his wind, and I won the prize and nothing was said about a foul. We rested a while and went at it anew. This time we clawed, bit, scratched and kicked. By accident my finger strayed into his mouth, and he nailed it, but by a sudden stroke I downed him and he let go. I was in a good way to win again, when his master rushed in and kicked me on the head, knocking me clear loose. Carnoviste drew his pistol and knocked the Indian down. Our men drew their weapons and the whole crowd prepared to fight. Things looked squally. Friendly onlookers brought about a compromise and nobody was killed, but Mexicano was not able to get up. I was very sore, but was able to ride races that evening. My party had the best horses, and we won, and soon the other party had nothing.

This Mexican, mentioned above, and I were out herding horses one day, and were on friendly terms with each other. He challenged me to shoot at a target with him, and we selected a cactus as our target. We shot until I won all of his arrows, and he got mad and said I had cheated him. He let drive at me and shot an arrow through my lower lip. I let him have an arrow in his breast, and he broke and ran towards camp. Two other Indian boys were watching our scrap and one of them came to me and helped to pull the arrow out of my lip, while the other Indian boy assisted the Mexican to get to camp. He soon recovered, and in a short time the band he was with left us, and I never saw that Mexican again.

CHAPTER XV

TRADING WITH MEXICANS AND RAIDING

We journeyed southeast and met a large party of friendly Mexicans with pack burros well laden with flour, meal, coffee, sugar and little trinkets to trade to the Indians for horses and mules, and they camped with us for several days. The Indian boys and I would steal these burros and drive them several miles during one night and leave them near water, then go back and the warriors would give us a plume or a red string and we would feel well paid for our night's work. When the burros got fat we would kill them and eat them. Sometimes the Mexicans would hire us to look for their burros, and they would give us blankets and trinkets for finding them.

When the Mexican traders left us we were what you would call, nowadays, "busted," that is, we had nothing left but the bitter end of a guilty conscience, so we had to go immediately on a stealing expedition.

We came down a river, I think it must have been the San Saba, but of course I do not know. I can only tell by the looks of the country since I came back to my people. We stole a small bunch of horses. We had come in afoot, and had secured enough horses to mount each Indian. There were thirteen Indians in our party, and we were traveling at night, going up the river, when we were fired upon by some men in front of us. We were in a narrow canyon, with the river on one side of us and a high bluff on the other side of us, and our enemies were hiding under the bluff. We scattered and some of us rode right through the attacking party and made our get-away. Not an Indian was wounded or killed, but one of our party, Chinava, was hurt by his horse falling with him. The night was very dark and the fire from the white men's guns blinded us. Some of our horses ran into a deep gully, but we all managed to escape. Several of our warriors who were at the rear when the firing commenced, managed to steal past the palefaces after the firing ceased, and we were all scattered and separated. Presently I heard the hoot of an owl, and I knew the signal, and in a very short time we were all together again and hastened along on our journey.

Next day, just before sundown, as we were nearing the Kickapoo, we discovered two men in camp with a large herd of horses, forty or fifty head. We concealed ourselves and watched them until nightfall; saw them round up the herd, and prepare to spend the night there. Just as the moon

rose we rushed into the camp, stampeded the horses
and started them on a run in the direction we were
traveling. The two men were asleep, and as we
rushed by their pallet we shot at them, but I do not
think we hit either of them. We wanted their
horses, and we got them. We kept those horses
in a run all night, changing mounts frequently, and
when the sun came up the next morning we were
many miles from there, and still going strong. In
the late afternoon of that day we discovered a party
of Rangers on our trail and we whipped up the
herd and kept going, and for four days and nights
we rode without food or water. I got so tired and
sleepy that I fell off my horse exhausted. The Indians picked me up and lashed me to a new horse,
and on we went.

The Rangers kept to our trail and we dreaded an
encounter with them. We did not know it at the
time, but immediately following the Rangers who
were pursuing us came a band of Kiowa Indians,
about twenty-five in number, who were watching
the Rangers and intending to steal their horses when
they went into camp, but they did not get the opportunity. Finally we lost the Rangers, and
thought ourselves pretty safe, and at a late hour
of the fifth night of the pursuit we lay down for
a short rest, not knowing that off to our right,

CHAPTER XV

about a mile distant, General McKenzie and a large body of soldiers were encamped, and sound asleep. The Kiowas, coming along, discovered the soldiers' camp and charged it and succeeded in driving off fifty-six head of cavalry horses. We were aroused by the shooting and the yells when that fight started, and we hastily mounted and started on our way with our herd, knowing that our own safety depended on flight, for we knew not who was engaged in battle in our vicinity, and we had no time to ascertain. After sunrise next morning we discovered a running herd of horses and Indians following, and with the aid of a small mirror one of our party had we flashed a ray which caught one of the Kiowas square in the eyes, and he in turn signaled across to us, and we knew that band of Indians were our friends, and within an hour's time we had joined forces with them. We went on across the plains together, and finally separated, the Kiowas going west to their headquarters in the Yellow House Canyon, and we to our village away up on the plains, beside a great lake of water.

Some time after this a party of about fifteen warriors, myself included, went down on the Pecos on a stealing expedition, and we came across some Mexican traders, who were coming up a draw with their burros loaded with their wares. We stampeded the Mexicans and captured the burros, and helped ourselves to blankets, powder, lead, caps, and other articles we wanted. We were highly elated over our easy victory, when we were greeted by a shower of rocks and missiles from a hillside above us. One of our party was struck on the shoulder and knocked from his horse. The Mexicans had slings, with which they were hurling rocks at us. We fired at them as they would show themselves, and pretty soon they let us alone and disappeared. If we killed any of these Mexicans I do not know it.

In the late fall of 1872 or 1873 our band decided to leave the plains and go across the Rio Grande into Mexico to spend the winter, because it did not get so cold in that region, and there was an abundance of wild game to sustain us. Just before we reached the Rio Grande we overtook another party of Apaches who were going to Mexico, and we joined forces with them. They had their squaws and camp equipage and so did we. In this party I found a Mexican boy who had been raised by the Indians and whom I had known previously. His name was Salito. My chief, Carnoviste, did not accompany our band on this excursion, but had gone up into the extreme northwestern part of Texas to look for another bunch of our tribe. However, he came into Mexico and joined us before the middle

CHAPTER XV

of the winter, bringing with him some more Apaches. While we were down there the Mexican boy, Salito, and I were often together and became great friends. We decided to steal away from the Indians and make a raid on our own hook. We slipped off afoot and soon got lost in the mountains away from food and water, but we found a little stream, and down in a canyon we saw a colt grazing. Salito went down and drove the colt up the canyon and I killed it with an arrow. We lay around there and ate colt for several days. We skinned this colt and made each of us a water bag out of the hide, and filling these water bags with water, we cut what flesh off the carcass we could carry and journeyed on down the Rio Grande, and somewhere near Laredo we undertook to swim across the river, but the stream was swift and full of "suck holes," and Salito came near drowning. But I managed to help him get out safely. Just as we landed we discovered two Indians and started to hide, but we soon learned they belonged to our own band. We found ourselves near a large town on the Texas side of the river, and that night we went into that town and stole thirty head of horses, Salito and I getting sixteen of that number. We reswam the river, and with the two Indians reached our camp safely in about ten days.

TRADING WITH MEXICANS AND RAIDING

Some time after this a party of our warriors made a raid into the interior of Mexico. I went along with this party and so did Salito. We went into a town one night to steal horses and discovered five horses tied in a stable, but the Indians were afraid to undertake to get them, so they sent Salito and me in to bring them out. The Mexicans were watching, and closed in on us, and shut the stable door and thought they had us trapped, but I jumped out through an aperture in the wall and got away, while Salito fell into their hands. I failed to locate my Indian companions, as they had departed somewhat hurriedly, thinking I had been captured, so I headed for headquarters afoot, and after traveling four days without anything to eat I accidentally found them. I had stopped at a spring to rest, when these Indians came in driving a bunch of Spanish ponies which they had stolen. They were surprised to find me there, and gave me a horse and we proceeded on to our village. Salito finally succeeded in escaping and returned to the Indians several weeks later.

The Mexican soldiers began to make it hot for us down there and we decided to drift back toward our old hunting grounds. One day a large party of these soldiers were reported to be advancing upon our camp and we hurriedly gathered our belongings and started on our return. When we reached the Rio Grande that stream was on a big rise and we had to swim across. We made a kind of a boat out of a stiff buffalo hide and put all the papooses into it. The craft floated all right, and with several Indians at each side it was ferried across with its live cargo in safety. It took us all day to get across. We lost one man.

We traveled four days and nights and then stopped in the roughs and rested. We made breastworks and prepared to fight the Mexicans, for we were sure they would follow us. Sure enough they came on and in a force outnumbering us five to one, but we met them bravely and drove them back. Carnoviste made a speech, saying, "If there is a warrior here who will forsake his dying comrades, quit his wife and children, and leave his hunting ground in the hands of the enemy, let him go now. The enemy is well armed with guns, but we are protected by the nature of our place; we have plenty of water and food enough to last us a moon. We cannot leave because our horses are given out and must have rest; at this time to escape by flight is impossible. If there are cowards among us, let them go now. In a few minutes the enemy will be so close that escape will be impossible. Let us fight together, and be assured that no force that the

Mexicans can raise can rout us from here." Not an Indian attempted to escape. All resolved to live together, fight together and conquer together.

The Mexicans made a furious charge, but were repulsed; up they came again, but fell back before our deadly fire. This time they seemed determined to take our camp, and many of our warriors were killed, but each one let his strength be felt in the line of the enemy. Carnoviste cheered the braves as the battle progressed. Night came on, and the Mexicans withdrew. We had sixty-two dead and many wounded. We buried the dead in a cave near by, killed their horses and dragged them in, too, and then filled the mouth of the cave with rocks. One warrior who was killed in the fight owned a Mexican boy. We killed the boy and buried him with his master.

The Mexicans did not renew the attack next morning. I do not know whether it was on account of their losses, or because we were in the United States. Our whole camp was in grief. The squaws would beat their breasts and cut great gashes in their arms, and their wailings were truly piteous. These were sad scenes, and civilization cannot comprehend the suffering, woe and misery of them. All was one continuous wail and lamentation. There was neither sleep nor rest that night.

CHAPTER XV

We carried our wounded on a litter made of two poles fastened on each side of a horse's shoulder, and the other ends on the ground. The poles were long enough to be springy. Withes were tied between these poles behind the horse, blankets were spread over them and the wounded Indians laid on and closely bound. There was a horse and litter for each wounded Indian. We came on north far enough to be out of the way of the Mexicans and joined another party of Apaches.

CHAPTER XVI

WE ARE KEPT ON THE MOVE

When springtime came we went near Fort Griffin and there stole six head of horses. The soldiers followed us. We went until we struck the trail of some Lipans and Apaches, and followed this trail for some distance and then scattered. The soldiers followed the other trail of those friendly Indians, who, having done no devilment, were not afraid. They supposed that the soldiers would just carry them back to the reservation, so they made no resistance. But not so. The soldiers rushed into their camp and murdered men, women and children, and only a few squaws escaped to tell the tale. Thus the innocent were persecuted while the guilty ones went free.

We pulled away from such dangerous territory and in a day or two came upon some Mexicans encamped in a canyon, and made a dash at them. They left everything and fled, but we overtook them and returned to their camp with their scalps dangling from our belts. We took what we wished and destroyed everything else. Word came to us that the Comanches and Kiowas were fighting the soldiers and wanted our help. We soon joined them and found the soldiers were entrenched in a great ditch. We cut them off from their commissary and tried to starve them out. Reinforcements came, but our scouts saw them and we escaped before they got there.

We again made for Mexico, for we knew that the soldiers would not follow us there. Down near the Sand Hills we met a party of Comanches. Food was scarce, and we went many days on short rations. We reached the Pecos, and in crossing that turbulent stream an Indian girl's horse gave out and she went down the river. I jumped in to catch her, and she caught me around the neck and I could not get loose. In desperation I struck her and knocked her senseless, then caught her by the hair and swam to the bank with her, and the Indians pulled us out.

Here we prepared a camp for the women and children. Some Comanches came up and we all left the families there, recrossed the river and started to make a run on the palefaces. We came to near the head of the Llano River, where we separated, the Comanches going further north, while we went down the river. We saw two men with an ox-team and made a dash at them, but they fought us back until they had a chance to run to a house nearby. We prowled around and waited for them to come out, but they did not show themselves.

WE ARE KEPT ON THE MOVE

Two or three nights later we slipped into a small town, and peeped into windows and saw many pretty things. We came out north of the town and discovered two men camped under some live oak trees. We killed and scalped them and stole six horses. I think these men must have been freighters. Northwest of there we found a spring, and one of the Indians lay down to drink when we heard the report of a gun. The Indian who was drinking howled with pain. We thought the Rangers were upon us, so we stampeded, and hid behind rocks and trees and prepared to fight. The Indian at the spring remained there, so Carnoviste cautiously stole back and found that this Indian's pistol had struck a rock and was accidentally discharged, striking him in the knee and inflicting a painful wound. This Indian became a cripple for life.

We traveled leisurely along going back, for we were not followed. One day we came in sight of four men on horseback, leading a pack mule. We rode down upon them and they separated. We finally ran them down and killed and scalped them, taking their pack and animals. In the pack was a large quantity of money, greenbacks and silver and gold. The greenbacks we tore up, but made ornaments of the silver and gold. When we reached our camp we had a big feast and dance.

CHAPTER XVII

GLIMPSES OF INDIAN CUSTOMS

We began preparations for a great festival, the significance of which I do not know. We first had to undergo a seven days' fast, then seven strong, robust Indians were selected to dance continuously for seven days and nights without partaking of any food, except a moist root prepared especially for this ordinance. The medicine men performed many jugglery tricks that I don't yet understand, and no others could, such as sticking knives into their bodies without bringing blood. I have seen them cut great gashes in their legs and no blood would flow. Then they would eat small apples that grew on a cactus found only in the mountains of Mexico, and of great value among the Indians. They made a preparation from these apples called "hoosh." We all ate nothing but "hoosh" for four days, and we felt so light and happy that we loved everybody and wanted to fly away. There is a plant which grows in Mexico which is called peyote, and is held in great veneration by the Indians, and it is quite possible that the medicine men used this in the preparation of the "hoosh" also.

Some of the medicine men claimed to control the atmosphere and command the rains to come. I

"MONTECHEMA"
Herman Lehmann in war garb of Comanche

have seen them go out on a high point and wave a cow's tail and chant for rain, and if it failed to come they drew the conclusion that some of their people had provoked the Great Spirit. Once I knew of them vainly trying, but the drouth continued, so the medicine men came into camp and placed the blame on a Mexican who was staying with us. This Mexican was firmly bound, hand and foot, with rawhide, and carried away upon the mountain and bound to a flat rock, and near him was staked a large rattlesnake. The snake was placed just near enough to strike the Mexican whenever he moved. We returned to camp and the incantations were repeated and there came a regular waterspout. Our wigwams were washed away, one white child captive was drowned, several horses went down in the raging torrent which rushed down the arroyo on which our camp was situated, and we had to flee to the mountain for safety.

Indians could forecast the weather by the webs of spiders. In dry weather the web was thin, long and high, but just before a rain the web was low, short and thick.

One morning an Indian put on an antelope skin and went out on his all fours to surprise and kill an antelope. He crawled out to within a hundred yards of where the fleet-footed animals were grazing. Another Indian saw this animal away off by himself, and not knowing that it was an Indian, he took aim and killed the disguised Indian. He went back to camp in grief and told what had happened. As the dead Indian was a relative to Carnoviste he started to kill the Indian, but the squaw of the deceased stepped in between them and saved his life.

A kind of snake infested that region something like the asp. Its bite was almost sure death. These snakes nearly always went in pairs, and if you killed one its mate would trail you up and bite you, even though you were miles from the dead mate. It was told me that a young Indian who had just married killed one of these snakes and traveled on and camped that night with his young wife. The snake's companion trailed him up, and just as the moon was straight overhead this serpent pierced its fangs into the throat of the Indian bride and she died immediately. The Indian quit the tribe and spent the remainder of his life hunting and killing these snakes.

Once we were encamped on a little sandy creek. The grass was high and dry. We smelled fire, and looking up we saw a great cloud of smoke. The prairie was on fire. We went to work pulling grass and clearing it away and burned all around our camp to check the fire and prevent it from reaching us. The blaze reached out fifty feet with its great fiery tongue, and the smoke almost stifled us. Some of our horses broke away and were lost. Snakes, deer, antelope, wolves and other animals rushed into our place of refuge. Thousands of animals perished in the flames; one old squaw's eyesight was destroyed, and many of the children succumbed to the heat.

CHAPTER XVIII

AN EXCITING RIDE

An Indian who was afterwards killed by the Comanches, whose name was Totoabacona, and I were out hunting one day. I was riding that noted dun mule and he a swift manageable pony. A buffalo made fight and took after old Dun and me. I spurred and whipped, but that aggravating mule was an established mule, and would not go until he got ready. The Indian would dart in and goad the buffalo with an arrow and for an instant detract his attention from Dun and I. He made one good shot, but the furious beast kept coming, so the Indian rode in between us and shot the buffalo, but so close was the ride the buffalo gored the horse. The buffalo staggered and fell right under the mule, and the pony ran a short distance and fell dead. I hitched the mule and went up to skin the buffalo, but the shaggy animal was not dead. He jumped up and made a dash at the Indian, but the redskin was too quick, and the animal tumbled over a small bluff, breaking his neck in the fall.

This little episode took place in the hills not far from a place where the mountains made a circle, enclosing a level prairie of several hundred acres and came within sixty yards of each other at the

foot on the south side. The slope was almost perpendicular, at least the ascent was impossible on
that side. It was a common pastime of ours to
head a drove of antelope for that natural amphi-
theatre and when they would go in we would form
a phalanx of warriors at the mouth and put some
of our boys on fast horses to give chase. When
they came near the mouth we would set up a yell
and close in at the point of attack and thus the poor
beasts would be compelled to circle and run themselves down and give up in utter exhaustion. This
was sport for the whole tribe, squaws, children
and all.

But these exciting drives make me think of another time when I fairly flew over very rough
country, seven or eight months after I was stolen.

The braves captured a large fat mustang stallion,
tied him down, blindfolded him, bound me securely
on him, and then several Indians mounted swift
horses. The stallion was then released. He looked
around and bit me on the arm; I forgot that I was
a stoic, and gave a loud yell. Just then the horse
took off across the plains and over the roughs,
jumping gullies and running for dear life. He came
to a deep ditch which he cleared at a bound. The
Indians followed but could not even keep in sight.
That stallion ran for about ten miles, and when he

CHAPTER XVIII

leaped another ditch he stumbled and fell to his knees, throwing me off. He was up with a bound and flitted away as lightly as he did the first mile, and I have never seen or heard of him to this day. I lay there, suffering with my arm, and chewing the bitter end of reflection, until one of the pursuing party came up to me. His horse was run down. Soon others of the party came up, and they laughed and cheered me, and bound up my arm. One took me up behind him and we went back to camp.

CHAPTER XIX

I FIND A GOLD MINE

While I was with the Apaches, Carnoviste decided to seek a new country. We were at that time in the mountains of New Mexico, the Guadalupe range it must have been. That region was getting pretty well crowded with Indians because so many of the Apaches having been pushed back by encroaching civilization. Carnoviste sent me and two Indians, Esacona and Pinero, to seek a new country far to the northwest. We started out in a southwesterly direction at first and went into old Mexico, where we did not find anything to suit us. After traveling many days our horses gave out and we stole fresh horses from Mexicans and took a northwestern course toward what I suppose is now Arizona. We captured a couple of burros and took them along to use in case our horses gave out, and in the event we could not find game we intended to kill and eat them. We came to a spring at the foot of a sloping mountain, where grass was good and game was abundant and there we camped for several days. Our horses had become jaded and tender-footed and we decided to leave them there until we returned, so starting out afoot and driving the two burros, laden with a good supply of venison

CHAPTER XIX

and waterskins full of water, we headed for an un-
known region that we had heard of, but which
none of our tribe had ever seen. We traveled along
leisurely for several days, going due west until we
came to a barren desert region, wholly devoid of
vegetation and water, just a stretch of white sand
for miles and miles. We had found water before
going onto this desert and we filled our waterskins
and prepared for a long journey across that unin-
viting wilderness. We plodded along for days, the
only thing to break the monotony was the fierce
sand storms which would occasionally sweep along,
blinding us and almost covering us and impeding
our travel. On the sixth day, far in the distance,
we discerned a chain of blue mountains, which at
first we took to be a low-lying cloud. We pushed
on, and as we went forward the mountains began
to take form and shape, and we knew that if we
could hold out we could reach them within another
week at the rate we were traveling, our speed being
necessarily slow because our two pack burros were
beginning to suffer for forage and water. Our
water supply was just about exhausted and we realized that if we did not reach those mountains we
would perish there on that desert with our faithful
burros. At last we reached the foot of those mountains on the fifteenth day after starting across the

desert, and so near exhausted were we that I believe if we had not reached there when we did we could not have held out another day. Going up a canyon a short distance we found a fine spring and an abundance of grass, and right there we stopped to rest for several days before penetrating those mountains. When we had rested for a reasonable time we pushed on and traveled leisurely into the very heart of one of the most beautiful regions I have ever seen. Game was in superabundance, black-tailed deer, bear, lions, panthers, and other wild animals were to be seen everywhere, and would not run when we approached. While we were prospecting in those mountains and happy in their solitude, we found a most peculiar formation, which arrested our attention, and we wondered at its grandeur. Near the top of a high mountain a kind of a tableland had been formed and from this tableland there was a sheer bluff or wall over which water poured when it rained, forming a basin many feet below. The wall over which this water flowed was worn smooth by the water's fall, and was of a peculiar blue rock formation. In the basin below we found a storage of clear water which had a mineral taste, and which we were afraid to use, for Pinero said it might be poison. In this basin we found the same kind of blue formation, and throughout the whole formation were outcroppings of a bright yellow ore which was in layers an inch or two in thickness and easily removed. Pinero and Esacona suggested that we get some of those pretty yellow and blue rocks to take to the squaws, and with our scalping knives we dug out a number of large pieces of the yellow stuff and put it in our packs and carried it away with us. I had several pieces of it four or five inches long and two or three inches in thickness. We noticed it was very heavy, while the blue rocks were rather light and full of pores. We had no idea what the stuff was, as we were all three just young Indian cubs and not versed in mineralogy, but when we got back to our village Carnoviste told us, when we showed him the pretty rocks, that it was gold, and that very thing kept our people from going into those mountains to establish our headquarters. Carnoviste said we would not be safe there, for where there was gold to be found the white man would hunt for it, and we were seeking a region where the white man would not come.

After spending one moon, or month, in those mountains, killing game, and selecting a location for our villages when the tribe was brought there, we took up the weary march across the wide desert and finally reached the former camping ground where we had left our horses, and we found them fat and in good condition, and after resting there a few days we set out for our headquarters, reaching there in due time and reporting to Carnoviste that we had found an earthly Happy Hunting Grounds where the Great Spirit dwelt in every canyon and where His smile kissed every mountain top at sunrise each morning. Carnoviste grunted his satisfaction and delight, but when we showed him the pretty rocks we had brought back with us, he sorrowfully shook his head, and said that inviting region was not for the Indian, that it would prove a delusion and a snare, and if we went there it would only increase our troubles, and we gave up all hope of ever finding a land where the white man would not come.

CHAPTER XX

CAPTURE A HERD OF CATTLE

One time a party of Mexicans came to our camp
to trade with the Indians. They had plenty of mescal, corn whisky, and tobacco, and most of the tribe
got drunk. One hundred and forty of the Indians
and sixty of the Mexicans went on a cattle raid, and
west of Fort Griffin, on the old trail, we ran into a
big herd being driven to Kansas. There were about
twenty cowboys with the cattle, and we rushed up
and opened fire. The cattle stampeded, and the
cowboys rode in an opposite direction. There were
enough of us to surround the cattle and some to
chase the cowboys, but they were not overtaken.
The second day we were overtaken by about forty
white men, who tried to retake the cattle, and in
the attempt two Mexicans and one Indian were
killed—the Indian shot through the neck—and we
had four horses killed. We repulsed them and got
possession of two of their dead, who were promptly
scalped. I do not know what other losses they sustained. We went on southwest with the herd, and
had over a thousand head when we reached the village. These we traded to Mexicans and immediately stampeded them. I remember some of these
cattle were branded HEY.

CAPTURE A HERD OF CATTLE

The scalps of the two cowboys were put on high poles and we had a big feast and war dance. We killed about forty of the beeves and roasted them. We kept up a chant and dance around those scalps all night. More Mexicans had come and replenished our stock of whisky. We had a little disagreement, and in order to settle the rucus satisfactorily to all concerned we killed two Mexicans and raised their scalps on poles. We drank all the whisky, sobered up, ran off the Mexicans and kept all their trinkets, guns, ammunition, etc., but they got most of the cattle, which was more than pay. Then we repented over the Mexican affair and hired them to make friends. We moved our village away out to the Sandy Hills and spent some time hunting. There we found deer, antelope, javelinas, and some few buffalo.

I have often been asked how we made the flint stone arrow spikes, and I will here endeavor to explain the process: We threw a large flint stone, from two to six feet in circumference, into the fire. After the stone became very hot, small thin pieces would pop off; we selected those pieces which would require the least work to put into shape, and picked these hot pieces up with a stick split at the end; while these pieces were very hot, we dropped cold water on those places we wished to thin down; the

CHAPTER XX

cold water caused the spot touched to chip off, and in this way we made some of the keenest pointed and sharpest arrows that could be fashioned out of stone. Many of these arrows in perfect shape can still be picked up in certain places all over Texas.

We sharpened our arrow spikes, mended our bows, and brightened up our guns. Our arrows were made of a straight dogwood withe, with a feather grooved in one end, and a flint rock or steel spike on the other. We first used flint rock for spikes, also flint rock knives, which were used to skin buffalo and other animals. Later when the soldiers began to come onto the plains, we found old barrel hoops and other steel around their camp, and from this steel we made steel arrow spikes, and discarded our old flint rock spikes. The Mexicans furnished us files with which to fashion and sharpen our arrows. For bowstrings we used sinew taken from the tenderloin of a beef or deer. In a separate quiver we carried a few poisoned arrows to use in battle. The venom of the rattlesnake was used on these spikes.

We started out south to make another raid on the whites, and the first thing that broke the monotony of the raid and stirred up a little local interest was several men near the Concho River. We had a fierce fight with them and lost three of our braves.

CAPTURE A HERD OF CATTLE

We put some sticks up in a big live oak tree, laid the dead up there (so the wolves would not eat them) and covered them with blankets. All of their guns, arrows, and trinkets were wrapped up with them and their horses led under the tree and shot, so the Indians would be mounted and equipped when they reached the happy hunting grounds. I do not know what loss the white men sustained, as we had no means of finding out.

We traveled southeast to another river and spied a man walking round and round. The Indians crawled up, waylaid him and sent an arrow right through his breast. He stood there and spit up blood. The Indians let him suffer a little while and then dispatched him and carried along his scalp. This man must have been lost, for he had nothing with which to fight, but he had some rusty knives and bundles that looked somewhat worsted from the weather.

Keeping our course we came upon some men working in a rock quarry. One man was guarding the camp. We surrounded them and fired twice at the guard and he ran and hid in the chaparral. The workmen made their escape through the thick undergrowth, and we took possession of the camp, where we found only one horse, five 44-calibre rim-fire Winchesters, with belts full of cartridges,

CHAPTER XX

sugar, flour, salt, and other things necessary for camp life. We destroyed everything we could not carry along.

We went south from there, as well as I remember, and saw some children playing in a field near a house. We slipped up close and made a run at the children, and Snapping Turtle, a Kiowa, grabbed at one child as he ran through the fence. A white man came out with a Winchester and shot Snapping Turtle through the knee. We fought there for about two hours and tried to get revenge, but the man was brave and cautious and we never got a fair shot at him. There were cattle near the house which bore a brand resembling a broadaxe or hatchet, but we did not want cattle; we wanted blood. We went on a little further and rounded up nine good horses. We sent these, the wounded Indian and two companions back to the village.

Further on we discovered a man making rails. When we rushed at him he threw down his axe and lit out for his horse, which was tied to a tree. He hastily mounted the animal and forgot to untie him. He spurred the horse into a run and when he reached the end of the stake rope the sudden stop caused horse and rider to turn a flip. The man got up running and made his escape, while we got the horse, a little sorrel pony. We rode up the hill and captured twelve horses, a big bay mule and a light sorrel mule. We then started for home by way of Kickapoo Springs, and there we made ourselves the present of a nice drove of fat ponies. But our scouts informed us that the hateful Rangers were on our trail. We dreaded those fellows, so we made for the plains, and traveled three days and nights without eating or sleeping. We well knew how sleepless and restless those Rangers were and how unerring their aim when they got in a shot, so we outrode them. On the fourth day we came upon a big old fat jackass some Mexicans had set free, so we butchered, roasted and ate him. He was very palatable after our three days' fast. We rested there and grazed our horses. Two days later we killed and ate a mustang. We thought we were out of danger, so we became a bit careless. We had started at daylight that morning and about a half an hour by sun the Rangers unexpectedly came upon us from the east. The chief ordered us to stand and fight, saying there was no hope in flight.

CHAPTER XXI

FIGHT WITH THE RANGERS

I learned, after my return to civilization, that this party of Rangers was commanded by the famous scout and Indian fighter, Captain Dan W. Roberts, who at this writing (May 27, 1927) is still living at Austin, Texas. In spite of the orders of our chief, when the fight started our men scattered, and only four of us remained to fight the trained Rangers. Some of the Ranger force followed a retreating Indian, whose horse's leg was broken by a shot, and he jumped up behind Mockoash, a Lipan who was with our party, and they ran away. The fleeing Indians carried our rim-fire Winchesters with them. Another Indian, a brother to my chief, was unhorsed and he ran west. I rode up beside him, and he jumped up behind me, and we made for our comrades, but the Rangers were too quick for us, and cut us off, and those who were after Mockoash and his companion turned on us, placing us between two fires. Nusticeno was the name of the warrior behind me. He protected us on one side with his shield, and I held my shield on the other side. I directed my arrows to those in front and he sent his shots backwards. Several bullets hit my shield and knocked it against my forehead, each stroke raising a bump, and I could hear them fairly raining on Nusticeno's shield. In a few moments my horse was shot down and he fell on me. Nusticeno had broken his bow, so he seized mine and ran for life. I implored him not to leave me, but he heeded not my entreaties in his mad scramble for life. I was pinned underneath the dead horse, and it seemed as if I would have to stay there and accept my fate whatever it might be. I lay perfectly still, when two or three Rangers dashed up, and one of them pointed his gun at me and I thought my time had come. I closed my eyes, there was a loud report, and it seemed to me I felt a bullet graze my temple. Two Rangers began talking, and opening my eyes I saw they were looking at me and from their actions they must have discovered I was not an Indian. They both dashed away after Nusticeno, and I could hear them firing at him. I listened to the firing until I thought they were out of sight, and then I scrambled out from under my fallen horse and crawled some distance on my belly and hid in the grass. After a little while the Rangers came back to look for me. I could hear them ride about and talk, and for a time they were quite near me. I lay still in a slight depression, with the high grass pretty well covering me, hardly daring to breathe for fear they would find me there.

CHAPTER XXI

They stayed on the battleground and searched for an hour or more, and finally left, going east. I remained in my hiding place until they were entirely out of sight, then I raised up, arose, and cautiously surveyed my surroundings. I went to my dead horse, but all of my weapons had been taken, and I had nothing with which to supply myself with food. My comrades were all gone, either killed or flown. I went to where Nusticeno was killed and came upon his corpse, about six hundred yards from where we were dismounted to fight. He had been scalped, and I thought skinned, from all appearances, and all of his weapons taken. I viewed this weird spectacle a few seconds and turned and ran until I fell breathless and exhausted to the ground.

We had with us at the beginning of this battle a little Mexican boy, and when the Rangers came near he quit the Indians and ran toward them with uplifted arms. They carried him away with them.

After resting and collecting my wits I realized that I was a long distance from my Indian headquarters (about 300 miles). There I was with nothing on but a buckskin jacket, and no way of providing myself with food. I started on the Indian trail, walking day and night, subsisting on grasshoppers, lizards, bugs, roots, and anything that I could find. I nearly starved for water. Finally I came to a small cave that contained water, but how to get it out was a problem. But I was so near starved I did not consider, so I crowded down into that cave head foremost, and by desperate effort squeezed myself between the rocks until I reached the water. After drinking my fill I found that I was fastened, and came very near drowning before I could get out of that tight place. I kept kicking and scrambling backwards until I succeeded in reaching the top.

I tramped wearily on, following the trail until I came to where the Indians had killed an antelope. The wolves had eaten all of the flesh that was left, but I sucked the bones and gnawed on the hide for nourishment. I ate prickly pear, and one day I was so nearly starved for water that I ate dirt where a mud hole had been formed by a recent rain. I became in a measure delirious, and when I came to my senses I was at a spring. I drank copiously, but I had starved so long the water would not stay on my stomach. I lay around there bathing my parched tongue in the water until I could drink a little. I stayed there that day and night. I was too weak and sore and faint to feel much pain. My sensibilities were dulled and the anguish of homesickness never bothered me. I recruited and recuperated there, catching a few frogs, which I ate raw, and considered them dainty morsels. I was loath to leave because I had nothing in which to carry water. I knew I could not remain there very long, so I went on and finally reached the village, and when I got there my toenails came off and I was sick for a long, long time.

Those Indians who ran when the Rangers came up had reached the village some days before I arrived, and had told that we were killed, and that they had killed our horses and buried all of our property with us. They told the chief of how I had turned back and taken his brother, Nusticeno, up behind me in an attempt to aid his escape, and great was the lamentation over our reported death. When I reached the village they were overjoyed to see me, and when I told how my three companions and myself had been forsaken by the others, the chief's anger knew no bounds. He made me a chief over all those who had deserted me, and I felt doubly repaid for all of my sufferings. They treated me kindly, made me a good comfortable bed, cooked my food nicely and showed me every consideration.

In order to make my honor complete, I told the tribe that I followed the Rangers and buried Nusticeno with his face downward and covered his last

CAPTAIN J. B. GILLETT AND HERMAN LEHMANN

Meeting for the first time since battle between Rangers and Indians, on the Concho Plains in 1873

resting place with rock so that the wolves or other wild beasts could not get him. (My! how they had shot that Indian! He was butchered terribly. There was no face on which to turn him. I can see that bloody form yet when I close my eyes.)

After I got well I could go ahead of a good many grown Indians. I could wear red strings and beads and lead the fight, and I was anxious to try my skill and bravery, but I was compelled to stay in camp nearly two months. We moved every few days to better hunting grounds and killed much game. Antelope were plentiful. The first thing we did when we killed one, was to go into the paunch and eat what we found there, then his heart and liver. We often feasted on wood-rats, pole-cats and opossums. We moved across the Rio Grande into the mountains of Mexico and there we killed bear, black-tailed deer and javelinas.

The Indians have a system of enumeration of their own, of which the human hand is the basis. They count upon the fingers until five is reached, when they denote the number by a hand. Six is a hand and a finger, and ten becomes two hands. But when twenty is reached a new name is used. Twenty is denoted by a man and forty by two men. Forty-five would thus be two men and a hand, and forty-six, two men, a hand and first finger, etc.

CHAPTER XXI

Before closing this chapter I want to refer again to the fight we had with the Rangers. Captain J. B. Gillett, who lives at Marfa, Texas, was in Captain D. W. Roberts' Ranger company when they caught us on the Concho Plains and engaged us in battle. In telling of this fight in his book, "Six Years with the Texas Rangers" (first edition), Captain Gillett mentions a white boy with the Indians whom he calls Fischer. I am the white boy he refers to, but he evidently had in mind Rudolph Fischer, who was captured in Gillespie County a year before my capture. As Captain Roberts, in his book, "Rangers and Sovereignty," also calls me Fischer, it is natural that Captain Gillett would make the same mistake. Fischer was captured by the Comanches, is still a member of that tribe, and now lives near Apache, Oklahoma. I was captured by the Apaches, and was with them in the fight mentioned. Captain Roberts and Captain Gillett both say the Indians they fought were Lipans, but I know they were Apaches, for I was with them. If they were Lipans, how came Fischer with them? These mistakes often occur in recording history and cannot be avoided. Captain Gillett mentions a Mexican boy the Rangers recaptured in this fight, who was stolen in Uvalde County. The boy had been with the Indians only a short time when the

Rangers got him, and had not learned to speak the Apache language very well. I was present in camp when the Apaches returned from a raid down into Southwest Texas and brought him in. He was taken along with our raiding party to wait on old Chinava, a brave Apache warrior.

Rudolph Fischer was a German boy, and was captured near Fredericksburg in 1869, I think, about a year before the Indians got me. He was adopted into the Comanche tribe, and after being with them about ten years he was brought back to his people near Fredericksburg, but he had become so thoroughly Indianized that he was not content to remain and resume the white man's ways, and after spending about a year with his parents, he returned to the Comanches, where he had a squaw and a child, and now lives on his headright in Oklahoma. Fischer became a very brave warrior and is held in high esteem by the tribe. I talked with Captain Roberts at my home in Loyal Valley, in 1881, after I was brought back from captivity, and we talked about the fight. He evidently forgot my name and having Fischer in mind, he wrote it that way in his book.

CHAPTER XXII

THE FIGHT ON THE CONCHO PLAINS

The following account of the battle on the Concho Plains in 1875, between Captain Roberts' Rangers and the Apache Indian band, of which I was a member, was related by Thomas P. Gillespie, and published in Hunter's Magazine in 1911. Captain J. B. Gillett gives a splendid account of this fight in his book, "Six Years with the Texas Rangers," but as space is too limited I will use only Captain Gillespie's account. At the time it was written Captain Gillespie was living at or near San Angelo, Texas:

"In August, 1875, while scouting in the upper San Saba Valley, we discovered an Indian trail on Scalp Creek, a tributary of the San Saba in Menard County. The trail was comparatively fresh and the indications were that it had been made by a band of twelve or fifteen Indians with a bunch of forty or fifty head of horses. Our command consisted of Captain Roberts, Mike Lynch, Jim Trout, Jim Hawkins, Ed Seiker, Jim Gillette, Andy Wilson, Henry Matamore, myself and a man by the name of Crump. There may have been one or two others whose names I have forgotten, but I think those mentioned were all that were present on this chase.

THE FIGHT ON THE CONCHO PLAINS

Our horses were in bad condition for a long pursuit but there was no alternative and we began the chase without delay. The trail led out across the head of Dry and Rocky Creeks in the north part of Menard County and on in the direction of Kickapoo Springs, crossing the Fort McKavett and Fort Concho road about nine miles south of Kickapoo Springs. It was nearly night when we reached this road and our horses being very much jaded and suffering for water, we left the trail and went to the springs, where we remained over night. As many of our horses had flung their shoes and were lame in consequence, we went to a ranch the next morning and reshod our stock, after which we resumed the pursuit. Some twelve or fifteen miles above the head of South Concho we again came upon the trail and followed it to the top of a mountain, where the Indians had halted and had removed the shoes from their stolen horses. Just why they should want to pull off the shoes from their stock has always been a mystery. Several theories have been advanced by Rangers and frontiersmen, but none hold good. These horse shoes were left where they had been pulled off, and in addition the Indians had torn two long strips from a blanket and had placed these strips in the form of a cross on the ground, and in this condition we found them. It

was about 2 p. m. when we discovered this sign on
the mountain, the weather was dreadfully hot but
we took up the trail and pushed on as fast as our
jaded horses could carry us. We knew from those
signs so familiar to a Ranger that the Indians could
not be far away and that they were moving leisurely along, and we hoped to overhaul them before
nightfall. We followed the trail, which led in a
southwest course, until we came out on the plains,
after which the trail led due west. About half an
hour by sun we came to a pond where the Indians
had watered their stock. The water in the horses'
tracks was yet muddy and the grass along the margin where the horses had come out of the water
was still wet, showing that we were close at their
heels. It being nearly night Captain Roberts said
we had better cook supper here and give our horses
a brief rest, which we proceeded to do, and after
supper we remounted and followed the trail as long
as we could see. It becoming too dark to distin-
guish the trail we lay by until dawn, giving our
horses a good rest, which they sorely needed. By
the time it was light enough to see we were in the
saddle, expecting every minute to come in sight of
the enemy. We rode at a moderately brisk gait
until about 7 o'clock, when Captain Roberts suddenly halted and said: 'Boys, I believe I see them.'

THE FIGHT ON THE CONCHO PLAINS

Far ahead in the plain we could see a few dark specks but not sufficiently to tell whether they were horsemen or other objects. Unslinging his field glass Roberts got a good view of them and said: 'Boys, there they are. They are riding slowly. They have not discovered us yet. Now you fellows follow close up behind me in single file. The sun is at our backs and by following my directions we can get close in on them before they see us.'

"We were all keen for the fight and our captain's orders were obeyed to the letter. We rode in the manner indicated and were within 600 yards of the Indians before they discovered us. There were eleven of them and as to numbers we were about equally matched. Besides the eleven, there were two riding along at a considerable distance to the left, and these two were the first to see us and gave the alarm. We broke rank and raised the yell—every man for himself, making full tilt for the savages. The Indians began rounding up the herd and mounting fresh horses, and when we got near enough to do execution they scattered and each sought safety in tall running. However, when we got in about 150 yards of them they rallied on a small elevation and opened fire on us. This was evidently for the purpose of giving some of their number time to catch and mount fresh horses. We killed three or four horses and probably killed or wounded an Indian or two before this crowd broke and ran. We carried Winchesters and needle guns, and every man in the company was a crack shot. A running fight followed and our men, singly or in pairs, selected their game and put in after them. The Indians scattered in pairs and when our men killed a horse the rider would hop up behind his comrade and continue the flight. Ed Sieker and Jim Gillette took in after two well mounted Indians, who, with their shields on their backs, were 'burning the wind.' After a run of 500 or 600 yards they brought down one of the horses, and as quick as a flash the Indian was up behind his mate and the race continued, until the horse ridden by the two Indians began to lose his wind and began to circle, a maneuver often practiced by the Indians when cornered under like circumstances. The boys had fired at least a dozen shots at these two Indians during this run, but on account of their shields had failed to bring them down. Seeing this circling ruse, Jim Gillette dismounted and with his needle gun took deliberate aim and broke the horse's neck, and then sprang back into his saddle and dashed forward alongside with Ed Sieker. When the horse fell, the Indian mounted on behind hit the ground a-running, still holding the shield over his back, while the horse in his fall had pinned the other Indian to the ground. The boys dashed up to the fallen horse and Gillette threw his pistol on the Indian lying pinioned under the horse and was in the act of shooting him when Ed Sieker shouted: 'Don't shoot him! Don't you see he is a white boy?' Gillette lowered his pistol and as a bare glance showed that the boy was closely held by the body of the horse and, even if foot-loose, he could not escape, they hurried on after the fleeing Indian, whom they overtook and killed after a race of about 300 yards. After having killed this Indian they tarried a short while to get his scalp and to gather up his bow, quiver, shield and other accoutrements worth carrying away as trophies, and when they returned to where they had left the boy under the dead horse, he was gone! At this they were puzzled beyond expression. The scene of the fight and the chase was an open plain with nothing to obstruct the view for miles, and from the moment the horse was killed until their return to the spot they had been in full view of the surroundings and the boy could not have gotten away without their having seen him make the start. There were a few scattering mesquites but none large enough to offer concealment. The grass was green and seven or eight inches high and into this he must have crawled off and secreted himself. The search began, and in a short time the entire company came up and all joined in the hunt. Every square rod for a mile around was gone over and every bush and tuft of grass was examined but the boy was nowhere to be found and we gave up the search as hopeless and went away completely mystified as to what had become of him.

"Some years later I learned that this boy was the captive, Herman Lehmann, who, when a child, was stolen from his parents in Gillespie County and kept nine years, during which time he became thoroughly Indianized, joined his adopted people in their wars and horse-stealing raids, but was at length restored to his mother and became, in the course of time, a good citizen.

"In this fight we captured thirty head of horses, which we drove to Mason County and delivered to their owners. At the first onset we crowded the Indians so close that in mounting fresh horses they had to abandon their saddles, which we captured, but being old and worthless we cast them aside."

CHAPTER XXIII

LOST IN A SNOWSTORM, RAIDS, ETC.

When winter set in we stayed in camp and recruited, fattened our horses and spent the time hunting. One cold day I was sent out to bring in the
horses. It was cloudy and began to snow. I went
on and lost my way. The snow came down thicker,
my horse fell into a sink hole and broke his neck;
I worked with him for some time thinking he might
get all right, but he died. By that time his tracks
had been obliterated. I wandered around through
the snow until night and continued to walk after
dark for a long, long time. At last I gave up and
lay down. I remember suffering so much with
cold as I lay there. Then I seemed to get warm,
and I thought it was all a dream. More nice deer,
buffalo, antelope, and other game appeared before
me and a good old squaw brought me some nice
warm roasted beef, then all went out. The next
thing I knew I was in camp, wrapped up in buffalo
meat. I then began to thaw; my fingers, toes, ears
and nose were badly frozen. I was rubbed with
meat until circulation started. Then I was placed
on a bucking horse and he would pitch me off; the
Indians would catch the horse and replace me on
his back. This was kept up until I caught several

113

hard falls. Then they dipped me in cold water and thoroughly rubbed me, placed me between warm blankets and gave me some nice fat meat. I was then allowed to sleep for a while. When I was awakened I was given a good meal of roasted buffalo hump, and after that how sweetly I did sleep. I soon recovered entirely.

Springtime came on apace, and when the weather got warm we made a raid down into the settlements for horses. I was left alone in a cedar brake for three weeks, but easily supplied myself with honey and small game. When they came back they brought with them a young warrior who had a badly sprained leg, caused by his horse falling with him. I took care of him while the other braves went east on a raid. When they came back they rewarded me with a pair of good horses and several ropes. We returned to camp, pretty well supplied.

We lingered around camp a while and then went down on the San Saba River on a raid; going on into Mason County, where we came upon a herd of horses. A man was pretending to guard them, but was fast asleep. We drove an arrow through him, and this aroused him for a few minutes, then he turned over into a sleep from which no man can awaken. We scalped him and drove off the horses.

We had just started when a man in a wagon drove up; we had a little fight with him, scalped him, left him in a dying condition and took charge of his team. It was then get away from there.

The next sport we had was slaughtering a man who was driving an ox team. We killed the oxen, sucked the paunch and lower intestines, stripped the colon with our hands, tied one end and filled it with water to carry with us. We ate the hearts, livers, lights and kidneys raw, while warm, and sucked the blood. We made a fire, roasted the ribs and had a feast off of those old oxen, while our scouts kept watch to see that we were not found by the whites. After resting here several hours, we traveled southeast for some distance until night overtook us. These stealing raids were not like jolly fishing parties or merry serenades, but silently and cautiously, swiftly, we proceeded, keeping our eyes and ears open.

We never feared Uncle Sam's regular soldiers much, for we knew they had to consume a great deal of time in getting ready to take our trail, but we dreaded the Texas Rangers and the frontiersmen, whose guns were always loaded and whose aim was unerring; they slept in the saddle and ate while they rode, or done without. When they took up our trail they followed it determinedly and doggedly

CHAPTER XXIII

day and night. We stole horses here and there, and started back to our headquarters. One fine morning we found the whole country full of soldiers, and had a desperate fight with them. Several of our men were killed. We escaped and hurried northward and met some Kiowas and Comanches, but our resting place was not here; we were driven into the Wichita Mountains, but even there the red man, the one to whom this country and all of its wealth and riches rightly belongs, could not stop even among the mountains. He must bow to the inevitable. He must give up to greater numbers, superior skill and improved firearms. Quanah Parker, of the Comanches, came out and persuaded us to come into the reservation at Fort Sill. Our men were rounded up and counted like cattle. Men came from all over Texas to examine and claim our horses. The white children in our possession were exchanged for squaws and children. Carnoviste said that as he had not lost any squaw he did not propose to give me up, and I did not want to go, for I had learned to hate my own people, so I kept hid. The Indians reported at headquarters that the Apache chief, Carnoviste, had a white boy in his camp, so the soldiers came to search for me. I was sitting in camp with Carnoviste when we saw the blue coats and brass buttons. I lay flat down and the Indians present threw blankets over me and sat down on them and silently smoked while the soldiers searched the tepee. One of the officers stayed around and talked and watched and smoked with the Indians. My nose and mouth were in the sand and I was mashed as flat as a horned frog and nearly smothered, but the Indians would have killed me before they would have given me up.

Our chief got mad because that officer stayed so long and asked so many questions, so he called his men together and decided to quit the reservation.

CHAPTER XXIV

WE RUN AWAY

Our men collected, the women and children came together, and we stole all of the horses, blankets and guns we could find, and under the cover of night we escaped. The next morning we were many miles from the fort and the detested whites. We made for the plains as fast as we could travel, and soon we were in our old haunts.

We needed horses, so a raid was ordered and a band of us went far down into the settlements. The first encounter we had was with two boys, on the James River, one nearly grown and the other smaller. They fought desperately, but were over-powered, killed and scalped. We stole many horses in that region, some of them, I afterwards learned, belonged to Welge, Stone, Ellebracht and Henry Keyser. We went to Fredericksburg that night, but we avoided killing anybody, for we were not anxious to be chased by the Rangers.

We then went on to the Packsaddle Mountain region. On Sandy Creek we saw a man chopping wood, and grazing near him was a sorrel pony with a saddle on. He saw us, jumped on the pony, and tried to get away. We crowded him closely, when he quit his horse, dropped his ax, lost his hat and made his way into a thicket. He soon left the thicket and ran to a house, and we saw him enter. We didn't often fool around a house when we knew there was a man in it, so we took his horse and went on down the creek. Near there we found and drove away twenty head of horses.

There came up a drenching rain, which wet our bowstrings, so we went into a thicket in the roughs and built a fire to dry them. We were thus busily engaged, when suddenly white men rushed in upon us. We stayed together and fought for a little while, but the Indians were falling all around, and we scattered. Going west, those of us who were not killed came together at a convenient place. Then we stole more horses and hurried on. We discovered that we were followed by the dreaded Rangers, who overtook us near the Concho on the second morning. We had a hard fight, and our loose horses were captured by the Rangers. One Indian was killed and several wounded, but we escaped.

We went on to where we had left our people in camp, but when we reached there we found they had moved. We found buffalo bones and on them pictures representing a fight with the white people. On some bones properly arranged were the pictures of seven men pierced with arrows, also a wagon burning up; the bones pointed northward. Twelve bones peculiarly arranged represented twelve days' journey. We traveled on for twelve consecutive days, then we could see smokes a long ways apart, all in rows pointing westward. This we took to mean that the Rangers were too thick and had made it so hot for the Indians that they had moved westward. It also indicated that they were closely pursued and warned us to watch as well as hasten to their rescue.

We went west for about one hundred miles. There was but little water in that country, but we knew where there was a spring. The white men pursuing our band proved to be soldiers instead of Rangers, and the Indians decoyed them off on a route where there was no water. We knew what the consequences would be, so at the spring we filled up our water bags and pursued the soldiers. Soon we began to find dead horses on the way, then we came upon a man nearly famished for water. He was stripped, scalped and cut to pieces. We followed and found eight others, and they shared the fate of the first mentioned. These soldiers passed close to the water, but it was in a deep hole, and the Indians kept it covered up. We saw from the direction the other soldiers were traveling that they would all perish on the dry sand, so we went back on the right trail of our people. We found them at the spring, but in a deplorable condition. All of their horses were jaded and worn out, and many of the squaws and children were afoot, and almost starving. Desolation, destruction and utter annihilation stared us in the face. Among the soldiers were some negroes, the first most of the Indians had seen. The Indians thought these negroes came from under the water, from the fact that our shadow always appears black in water. We called them "buffalo soldiers," because they had curly, kinky hair and heads like bisons. Our arrows would not penetrate their skulls. I remember hearing our chief instruct his warriors one time that in fighting the "buffalo soldiers" never to shoot them in the head, because the skull was too hard, and it would turn the arrows, mash the bullets, break spears, and dull lances, but to shoot him through the heart and kill him easy.

At this spring we rested, killed game and caught some mustangs. From here we went up to the head of the Pecos River, and on to the Rocky Mountains. Here we could take it easy and could lie down and sleep in peace. At first game was plentiful, but as we went on up into the mountains game became scarce and our horses had no grazing. We cut holes in our youngest horses' ears and started them down the mountains to live, but we kept all the old skinned-up mules to feed upon ourselves. The first one we killed was an old skinned-up gray mule; his back was one solid sore from being rubbed by the Indian saddle. We ate him and sucked his hide and bones to get all of the nutriment out. The sores were the first parts we ate. That was sweet and tender.

It began to snow, and there we were, in those cold and high mountains without fire, food or shelter. To go down on the sleet over those steep places, where the least slip would hurl us into eternity, was hazardous; to ascend higher was impossible, and to remain there meant starvation. We killed and ate all the mules we kept, sucked and fought over the hides and bones like hungry dogs, gnawed and chewed our own moccasins, and bewailed our condition. Here we had not the tenderhearted soldier nor the revengeful Ranger with whom to contend, but freezing and starvation were more horrible. We laboriously worked our way down and out of those mountains, and when we reached the valleys we found that many of our horses which we had sent down there had found good picking and were in good condition. We managed to kill some game and fared some better. After spending some time in that region we turned back toward our old hunting grounds. We had undergone so many hardships that most of the tribe had sickened of freedom, and wanted to go back to the reservation. A council was held and it was decided to go back and give up. The commissioners allowed us to move off twenty-five miles from head-quarters and live in our own camp, as we had come in of our own accord, so we were allowed more liberties than those of the tribes who were forced to come in and surrender.

CHAPTER XXV

CARNOVISTE IS KILLED

On this reservation it was easy to purchase whisky of the most villainous kind from traders, who would slip it in and sell it to the Indians, despite the watchfulness of the soldiers. The present-day boot-legging activities are of similar character, I think, and the liquor offered now is about on a par with the concoctions dispensed to the poor, simple savages. When a quantity of this liquor was brought into camp it always produced rows and fights. A great many old grudges and feuds were brought up between different parties of our tribe when we were drinking, and a fuss or a murder was sure to follow. One of these drunken brawls resulted in the death of my best friend and master, Carnoviste, and made me a fugitive from the tribe for good. After a general carousal one of the unfriendly bands came to where some of our warriors were and demanded fire-water. A fight ensued in which one of our braves was wounded in the stomach. In a few days we retaliated by going to their camp and helping ourselves to some "beer" there. A hard fight followed and one party or the other would have been annihilated if the soldiers had not interfered. Our party being the aggressors, we expected to receive the greater punishment, so our chief called together all of our forces and we decided to steal horses from the other band and run away again. But before going we decided to all get on a big spree, as some traders had brought us a good supply of fire-water. That carousal was the worst I ever witnessed. Squaws fell out and literally cut each other to pieces. One squaw, while drunk, proved untrue to her husband. He cut off her nose and made her go to the wigwam of the man who had taken advantage of her intoxicated condition, and there she had to remain. The couple were forced to camp on the outer edge of the village. Several squaws died from the carousal, which aroused the ire of their husbands and they began quarreling. A band of us drove another band back toward where the soldiers were quartered, and then a few of us gathered up our belongings and all of the liquor and started for the plains region. We traveled a day and night and made camp in a nice, cool, shady place, and were preparing for a real spree. Suddenly up rushed a dozen warriors of our own tribe, and attacked us. We would not double-team on our kind, so twelve of our braves volunteered to fight those twelve, but while they were preparing for the fight the enemy killed one of our party and ran back. Carnoviste ordered me to bend my shield and help drive away the cowards. He and I and several of our comrades mounted fast horses and gave chase. We ran them above five miles to where they had prepared an ambuscade, and very foolishly we went right into the trap. Indians seemed to rise up out of the ground and fire at us. All of our comrades were killed. We turned and retreated slowly, a kind of running fight, to within a quarter of a mile of camp. Two or three came up with us and we had a hand-to-hand combat. Lances, spears and tomahawks flew lively for a while, but I was too busy to take much notice of what was going on around me. A warrior raised his spear to end my days, but Carnoviste, seeing the movement, thrust him through with a lance. At the same instant a medicine man killed Carnoviste. A medicine man thinks he can't be killed, that he is proof against his enemy as long as he refrains from eating swine. I thought, too, that he could not be killed. When Carnoviste fell, this medicine man came toward me with a Winchester, and waving his shield. He said to me, "This is your last day, for now you die." I ran behind a big rock and replied, "You or me." I had nothing but a bow and arrows, but I was determined to put up the best fight I could and try to avenge the death of Carnoviste. The other warriors had hurried on to rout our camp, no doubt thinking the medicine man was more than a match for me. He shot at me two or three times, his balls being deflected by striking my shield. I ran around and around that big rock with the medicine man after me, confident of victory. I had always hated that old devil, for all during the time I had been with them he never lost an opportunity to torment me. But I was just a helpless captive boy, and could not resent his outrageous treatment of me. Now it was different, for my heart was filled with a hatred that was unleashed by the killing of my chief. I became cool and collected, and as I ran around the rock the fourth time, I suddenly turned and sent an arrow under his shield and through his stomach, and as he threw up his arms I let drive another feathered shaft which penetrated his side. He fell and asked me not to shoot any more, saying that he was killed. I was afraid that he was not quite so dead as he would have me believe, so I sent another arrow that pierced his heart, and he rolled up his eyes and died with a faint groan. Carnoviste was avenged! I picked up his shield, took off his belt and buckled it on myself, made myself a present of his Winchester and cartridges, and felt that I could then whip all of the party which had attacked us. I knew that the death of the medicine man would soon become known, but I was proud of my victory. I went to an elevated spot and sat down where I could see the warriors in camp. Could tell by their yells of victory that they had routed or killed all of my band. I could hear the shrieks and moans of the squaws. Finally I saw some of the warriors go out and find the body of the big medicine man, and then a howl went up. I concealed myself among the rocks on a mountainside, and although they searched diligently for me they did not find me. Night came on, and with it the realization that I was utterly alone in the wide world without a friend or protector, a hunted and hated thing to be slain on sight. My friends were all dead. Where could I go? The hill, or range of hills, which afforded me concealment swept around north of the main village, forming a half circle. The scene of the battle we had, in which Carnoviste was killed, was nearly due west of this village. Knowing that searching parties would in due course of time look for me, I bore away and followed the ridge to a point north of the camp or village, where I waited until near the hour of midnight. My only hope lay in flight, but whither? Just at that time the Apaches and Comanches were not on good terms, although a treaty had been made between

them some time before. Anyhow, I did not know
the Comanche language, and should I fly to them
they might kill me. But I made up my mind to go,
and at once, but before going I was determined to
slip into the village and have a talk with Carnoviste's sister, Ete. She had always been good to
me and I loved her dearly. And, by the way, this
same woman is still living, or was two years ago
(in 1925), when I had a letter (written for her)
asking me to come to see her once more before
she dies. She said she was almost blind, and is
very old. She lives on the Apache reservation in
New Mexico, among her tribe, the Apaches. You
may wonder why I did not go to see her. As much
as I would like to see this old woman again I did
not dare to go among that tribe, for there are yet
living certain warriors who would not hesitate to
avenge the death of the medicine man.

I told Ete how Carnoviste had met his death,
and how in turn I had slain his murderer. She
thanked me, and said she would never forget me,
but she urged me to fly from there. She gave me
blankets and provisions, and told me to go to the
herd and get a certain horse, which for endurance
and hardihood was considered the best of any owned
by the tribe. He was a gray horse, on which I had
won many races. With tears and sobs we bade

each other good bye, and I went to the herd. It was a trying hour to me, to voluntarily tear myself from old associations and customs and enter upon a life I knew not of. I silently gathered up my arms, ammunition and provisions, and cautiously crept up to the horses and selected the gray mentioned above, the swiftest in the herd. I would sooner have died than taken any other, for Ete's sake. I mounted him and struck out into—I little knew what. There I was isolated from the Indians and afraid of the whites—absolutely alone; not a friend, acquaintance, or even an enemy with whom I could speak.

In trying to secure the horse I had chosen I assumed imminent risk, and it was past the hour of midnight when I finally succeeded in getting the animal away from the herd. It required but a few moments to saddle up, mount and be off. I shaped my course eastward, and was many miles away when the morning sun came up. I found myself in a vast plain with a low range of hills far to the north. This plain was wholly without vegetation except cactus and sage brush. The soil was loose and sandy, and this gave me some uneasiness, since my trail would be easily followed by my pursuers. During the day my horse and I suffered from the effect of thirst, but in the evening we came to a creek, where an abundance of water was found. The sun was about an hour high when I reached this creek, and after having slaked my thirst I rode to a high ridge that lay a short distance east of the watering place. Just over this ridge I found grass in a small cove and here I dismounted to let my horse rest and graze a few hours. Leaving my horse there I went back to the crest of the ridge to keep watch, as the elevation enabled me to see a great distance in the direction from whence I came. The sun was low in the heavens, and I had not been on watch longer than half an hour before I discovered what I took to be horsemen, mere specks on the horizon, far away to the west and directly on my trail. Going back to my horse, I hastily mounted and resumed my journey, and that was the last I saw of my aforetime friends, the Apaches, for several months.

Before closing this chapter I want to say that one of the Apaches that stole me, a brother to Carnoviste, and who afterwards became a chief among his tribe, was not with our party when we had the fight, so he was not killed. This chief's name is Chiwat, and he now lives among the Comanches at Indiahoma, in Oklahoma. His picture appears elsewhere in this book. Pinero and Esacona also live there.

CHAPTER XXVI

I LEAD THE LIFE OF A HERMIT

After many days travel over arid plains, rugged hills and deserts, during which time I came near perishing from hunger and thirst, I came to a deep, narrow canyon in which there was a small stream of pure, clear water, and a growth of cottonwood trees along the margin. My horse had become exhausted, and most of the day I had led the faithful beast. The walls of the canyon were almost perpendicular in places, and I experienced some difficulty in finding a place of descent to the creek below. Finally I discovered a narrow trail leading down the declivity and when once in the canyon I found not only good water, but also an abundance of good grass, and here I took up my abode. How long I remained in this canyon I cannot say, but I must have stayed there six or eight months, perhaps longer. On my first coming I found deer tracks and the footprints of other wild animals, which made this little stream their watering place, and later I discovered that the game was quite plentiful. After a few weeks' stay in this solitude I became reconciled to my lonely life. I regarded all men as my enemies. In a friendly cavern in the walls of the canyon I found shelter and concealment at night, and as game came in to water near my place of hiding I had no occasion to wander beyond the narrow precincts of the canyon. But with all of this there was a sense of dread weighing on my mind, a presentiment of evil to come, a racking fear lest the abundance of grass should attract the attention of my enemies and that I should be discovered and slain.

And thus the days and weeks and months glided by, until one bright night I was startled from my sleep by a strange sound, just what it was I could not tell, but it seemed to have been that of a human voice. I went outside of my cave and listened, and in a few moments I heard a loud laugh! The moon was at its full and the canyon was lit up almost as bright as day. Going around a projecting rock near my cave and looking down the canyon I saw a large camp fire not three hundred yards away, and I could see human forms passing to and fro near this fire, and could hear voices.

Taking advantage of a growth of willows which fringed the bank of the little stream I crept up sufficiently near the camp to hear their conversation, and to my utter dismay I found that they were Apaches, and I knew every one of them. They were evidently returning from a raid down in Texas, as they had a large drove of horses, which were being herded below their camp in the canyon, having come in through the mouth of the canyon. Returning to my cave, I gathered up a supply of dried venison, secured my horse, and going up the canyon some distance to a gap that served as an outlet to a level plain above, I struck out toward the east, not knowing where I was going any more than on the previous occasion when I had fled for my life from the same enemy.

I rode for several days, and crossed a number of streams. On several occasions I saw men whom I took to be white men or Mexicans, but these I avoided, knowing that they would take me to be an Apache, the common enemy to all men. I was traveling southeast, keenly alert lest I should be surprised by white man or Indian. I was a wanderer on the face of the earth. I came to a stream and spent a while there. I would get bear grass and love vine and boil these in water until they became a strong ooze, and with that I would wash my hair, which grew long, straight and beautiful.

I had twenty-eight cartridges for my Winchester; every ball brought down a deer, antelope or buffalo. The ammunition lasted me quite a while, for in order to husband it I used my bow and arrow to kill game. When my cartridges gave out I carried the gun over between the Pecos and Rio Grande somewhere and hid it in a cave. I was afraid of the Mexicans, the Americans and everybody, so my gun was of no further use to me. I did hate to give it up, but then I knew where to find it if I ever needed it again. I guess it is there buried in that cave yet; I never went to see about it.

While in that region I found game very scarce, and I had to eat cactus apples, and sotol, and other vegetation. I went north and my food and water gave out entirely. I saw a drove of antelope, but could not kill any, so I went seven days without food and water. I was just about ready to give up, to lie down and die, when I found a skunk. I killed him, cooked him and ate him, but I was careful not to eat too fast or too much at once. I did not waste any part of him, for food was too scarce. I soon found some muddy water. I put grass over it to keep from drinking flies or bugs; drank water, watered and rested my horse, ate more polecat, drank more muddy water, and felt much refreshed.

I traveled on and found some buffalo, and selected a small calf and roped him. I jerked the little fellow down and dragged him a short distance, then thinking I could manage him, I jumped down to cut his throat, but the little fellow got up and butted me down and ran over me. I got up, but down he brought me again. I drew my bow, but never tried to get up. I had fifty arrows; all these I stuck into that little buffalo, but I was so weak I could not kill him, and he kept butting me around. I finally managed to get to my horse and climbed on, and rode off, the buffalo calf being still attached to the end of the lariat. I dragged him until he was no near dead that I could get down and finish him. And right there I had a sure enough feast. I cut the calf open, and as usual ate the warm liver, and from his paunch I drank the sour milk that I found there, then I took a good rest. Later I skinned and dressed this calf, ate more of the entrails and prepared for cooking some meat. I got two dry sticks and rubbed and rubbed them together, cut new notches in them and rubbed on, but I was so weak I thought the fire would never come. By persistent effort I saw a little smoke. I blew on that end and soon a spark was visible, then a blaze. I was very careful not to have much smoke.

When I cut the meat I was cautious not to offend the Great Spirit. If an Indian cuts or punches a hole in a piece of meat before or while he is cooking it, he has offended the Great Spirit, and is sure to have some misfortune on the trip. If anybody in the camp with Indians pushes a stick through meat to cook it, he is immediately banished from the camp, if not killed.

I adhered to all of the superstitions, for I believed in them, as I was taught to do. I ate all I could, smoked, moved camp, ate, smoked and moved camp again. At night I put my meat under my head and soon fell asleep. I did not tie my horse, for he would not leave me. In the night I heard him snort and run up near me. I grabbed up my meat and other equipments, and jumped on him and rode away. These night moves were nothing unusual for me. I was soon sure nobody was after me, so I dismounted and fell asleep, but again I was aroused, and this time I saw what the trouble was. A big lobo wolf was smelling under my head for the meat. Of course I thought of Indians dressed in the skins of wolves to get close to me; I bounded up and let drive an arrow which ended that wolf's career, then turned around and shot another and another, until I had killed five, and several ran away.

CHAPTER XXVII

I MAKE A SADDLE

I soon found myself on the buffalo range proper, and food was plentiful, but the saddle I had (made of a forked stick) hurt my horse's back, so I concluded to make a better one. I tanned and dressed some hides. Fortunately I had a file and a piece of steel among my possessions; I cut a pole and fastened this steel on one end, and set the other end of the pole in the ground. I rubbed the fleshy side of the hide over that steel until all the meat was worn away. Then I would put brains of the animal on the hide and that would make it soft and pliable. This was a slow process of tanning, but I had more time than anything else. I cut down a willow tree, hacked off a fork and whittled out a saddle tree, covered it with rawhide, padded it with buffalo hair, recovered this and then put on the extras, such as stirrups, etc. I bent a willow stick around and covered it with hide and made good stirrups. I then covered the whole saddle with buffalo robes and let them extend down as fenders. I measured my horse's back, and made everything fit. I was a long, long time working, changing and fitting this saddle, but my labor and perseverance rewarded me with a saddle that fit superbly and rode comfortably, and which was indeed quite a curiosity.

I tanned hides from the buffalo to the blacksnake and made moccasins, my file serving the purpose of an awl with which to sew, and sinew was used as thread.

I wound around, constantly shifting my position, until one day I came in sight of a town, and I saw two men riding along. I turned and rode the other way as fast as my horse could carry me. I rode out toward the Pecos, and one day I killed a bear, made a fire and had a fine roast. I got a good greasy meal that time.

I usually picked my grounds, staying in rough places, but never where I could be hemmed up. I was then in my sixteenth year. I would lie down at night and spend hours watching the great celestial panorama, the thousands of bright orbs, enclusterings and configurations of exceeding beauty. I would look at the great starry vault, this blue dome, and then at my shield, and I would see that the larger stars occupied the same position on my shield that they did in the heavens, and thus on cloudy days my shield served as a compass as well as a protector.

I returned to the plains, our old haunts, and I would lie at a watering place and wait for antelope to come in to drink and then I would kill them. My horse was fat, for the grass was fine.

One night I could hear wild animals running, and the scream of something like a panther, but I did not think it was that kind of an animal. It didn't sound right. Then wolves began to howl, and they did not sound exactly right. I was pretty sure Indians were near, but the imitations were not of my tribe. I lay perfectly still, listening. Rattlesnakes seemed more numerous than usual, and I could hear them rattling all around. The whole animal world seemed to be disturbed. I silently secured my horse, threw on my equipment, and stole away in the darkness. Next morning I saw many Indian signs; I must have been close to a large party. I saw a horse that belonged to them, but I had quit stealing, for a horse other than my mount would be of no benefit to me, for there was no one with whom I could trade.

I rode out on the plains and worked away on my moccasins. I got out of reach of water and my food gave out. I hunted for game and searched for water for several days, and when I found the water I let my horse drink first, but I was careful that he did not take too much. I stayed at this water three days, and was loath to leave it. I went up on a high point nearby and saw Indians coming.

I MAKE A SADDLE

I ran and mounted my horse and got away from there without being discovered. So I went back to the buffalo country and there I tarried for quite a while, occasionally finding old camping places where white hunters had been, and about these old camps I was sometimes fortunate in finding articles which I could use.

I was becoming tired of this lonely life, and I decided to make friends with somebody, and suddenly the thought occurred to me to join the Comanches. I had met them frequently while I was with the Apaches, and although I could not understand their language I could make signs which they could understand, and after a while I believed I could master their dialect. I wondered what terms they were on with the Apaches, and how did they stand with the whites. Fully a year had passed since I had left the Apaches, and the two tribes may be at peace or war. In either event I decided to risk my chances.

CHAPTER XXVIII

I BECOME A COMANCHE WARRIOR

One morning I located a party of Indians, and soon discerned that they were Comanches. At a safe distance, and unobserved by them I followed these Indians all day, and watched them go into camp that night. I selected an hour some time after dark for approaching the camp, for I intended to make some investigations before revealing myself to them, for I did not know what kind of a reception I would receive and I wanted to play safe. So tethering my horse at a convenient distance from the camp, where I could easily get and mount him if I had to make a hasty escape, and taking my bow and arrows, I crept up close to the camp-fire and listened. The Indians seated around were talking and laughing, and seemed to be in high good humor. As a rule the Comanches are a fun-loving people and enjoy a good laugh, while the Apaches are morose and never laugh except when someone is hurt or some calamity befalls them. These fellows must have been telling some of their day's adventures, but I could not understand what they said. After remaining there within a short distance of them for twenty or thirty minutes, I mustered up enough courage to do a daring thing.

SALTPETER, A COMANCHE BRAVE

I BECOME A COMANCHE WARRIOR

I walked right in among them, unannounced! My
sudden appearance caused consternation. Letting
out loud war-whoops and yells, each brave sprang
to his feet, and darted off into the darkness, leaving
me standing in the firelight. I must have been a
vicious looking Indian—long dangling hair, un-
couth and unkempt. There I stood, wondering if
they would come back and try to kill me. Soon
they collected and came back in a charge, whooping and yelling, and I was surrounded in very quick
time. I made signs for peace, and tried to tell them
I was a poor lone Indian without a friend, and hungry. The few squaws who were there were the
first to approach me. One old woman, with a
fierce countenance and only one eye, came up close
to me and began to chatter in an excited voice, but
I could not understand her. I was wild, young and
timid, and I could not look that old she-devil in
the eye, which came near being my undoing, for
I afterwards learned that she wanted them to kill
me right there, saying I would bring trouble to
them. However, a young warrior came close and
began talking to me in the Apache tongue, and I
told him that I was an Apache from force of circumstances, driven from the tribe; that I had killed
a medicine man who had murdered my chief and
master; that I was a white man by birth, but an

143

Indian by adoption; that I loved the Indian and hated the white man; that on my shield were the scalps of whites whom I had killed in battle, and that I was regarded by my race as a mortal enemy; that I was a petty chief under Carnoviste and had had a small band of warriors of my own, but they were all dead, killed in a drunken brawl; that I had forsaken the Apaches for good, and they were at that very moment seeking to take my life; that I wanted to become a Comanche, and dwell with them and forever make war on the Apaches and the white people. I told them many things of which they knew, and another brave came forward and said he had seen me with the Apaches at a certain time, and that I had run a race with him and beaten his horse, and he knew Carnoviste and other Apaches. After hearing my story in detail, and which I told truthfully and without exaggeration, they told me I was welcome to stay with them as long as I pleased, and that I could accompany them to the main body of the tribe to which they were going the next morning, and they assured me that the big chief, Cotopah, would give we welcome there. Accompanied by two of the young braves, I went out and brought in my horse. The squaws gave me plenty to eat, fixed me a comfortable pallet, and for the first time in many months I felt that

I BECOME A COMANCHE WARRIOR

I was among friends, and I lay me down to sleep with a feeling of security and contentment.

The next morning my horse and I were the center of attraction, and some of the braves wanted me to run races with them. They wanted to trade for my splendid horse, but I would not part with him. He had been my sole companion during all of those lonesome months, and I was much attached to him. They offered me horses, guns, blankets, shields, and one old warrior offered me his daughter, but I remained firm in my resolve to keep my faithful horse.

We went on to the main body of the tribe, which we reached after several days' journey, and I was given a cordial welcome by the whole tribe when my story was made known to them. The chief called his warriors together and they held a council, and after asking me many questions, through an interpreter I was told that I would be taken into the tribe on condition that I would always remain a Comanche, that I would help them fight their enemies, and never surrender to the white men. I made them a big speech, in which I told them I was an Indian, I ate raw meat and I drank the warm blood of the wolf to give me the ferocity of that animal; that I poisoned my arrows with the venom of the rattlesnake to make sure that they would kill the hated white man when they sped toward him. My talk pleased them, and sitting in a circle we smoked the pipe of peace. After smoking we all stood up, and marching around we placed our right hands over our hearts and then raised them toward the heavens. This process began slowly, but as we marched we struck a lively step, striking our breasts repeatedly and raising our hands very much like the school children now do in modern calisthenics. This was kept up for some time no doubt to see how much I could endure and then I was led before the chief for a kind of an obligation, in which I promised faithfully to perform all the duties of a Comanche warrior, to help provide for, protect and defend those with whom I was entrusted and surrounded, and to obey my chief in all things, in peace and in war. Thus I was adopted into the tribe, and became a Comanche. I have remained a Comanche ever since, and those same privileges which were bestowed upon me in that solemn hour are mine to this day, and I am recognized by all Comanches as a tribesman, whenever I want to claim my tribe relationship.

I was given a Comanche name, Montechena, and that name appears today on the tribal records in Washington—Montechena Herman Lehmann.

I was allowed the privilege of selecting the family

with whom I was to live and become a member of, and after looking them over I selected Cotopah, who could speak Apache, as my brother, and I have never regretted my choice, for Cotopah proved himself to be a brother in many ways.

CHAPTER XXIX

MY FIRST RAID WITH THE COMANCHES

The Comanches seemed to have accepted me in good faith right from the very start, for within a short time the chief in selecting a party of warriors to go on a raid to the white settlements directed that I go with them. He asked me if I knew the country where we were going and I told him that I had often been there with the Apaches; in fact, that was in the region where I had been captured; that there were many good horses to be obtained there, all of which he knew, for he said he and his people had dwelt in that region for many moons before the white men came and took those hunting grounds from them.

Before starting on the raid it was decided to move headquarters and go north some distance. The squaws tore down the wigwams, packed them up, tied them on travois poles and we moved along, traveling leisurely and killing game, and drying meat. The Comanches kept out spies and guards similar to the Apaches, only the chief planned our routes, located suitable camping places, directed raids and fighting expeditions, and was general manager of everything, and when raiding parties were sent out the best medicine men stayed with the squaws to care for the wounded when they were sent home for careful nursing, while the Apaches always took their best medicine men along.

We were moving along peacefully when a signal came from the scouts, "prepare for trouble." No command was necessary; everybody understood the signal, and Indians are ever ready to wage war, no matter with whom or what. We rode out in advance of the squaws, everyone trying to be in front. We did not go far until we saw a Mexican train of wagons, who in the meantime had discovered us. We surrounded the wagoners, whooping and yelling and shooting. The Mexicans hastily abandoned the train and ran into a dense chaparral, and we captured two girls and a boy in the rout. We killed several of the Mexicans and took their scalps, then we examined the wagons and found them loaded with merchandise, taking all the tobacco, sugar, powder, lead, cartridges and guns we could find, as well as blankets and some clothing, and then set fire to the wagons. We hurried from there and traveled for about five days, and came upon a party of movers. They were pretty strong, so we did not attack them, but we stole all of their horses and left them afoot.

We journeyed on and found an ideal camping place, where we prepared to spend a while. The scalps we had taken were placed on poles and we had a big scalp dance, the squaws going to the left and the warriors to the right, dancing, yelling and shouting, continuing that day and night and part of the next day.   Then the plunder was divided.

For a while we hunted and killed an abundance of game, and supplied the camp with meat, and then the raiding expeditions were arranged.   We divided up into small squads and started out to steal.   The band I was placed with came down the Colorado, crossed over to the San Saba, and then to the Llano, stealing all the way.   Down near Packsaddle, in Llano County, we came up on a party of white men, who hid under a bluff and rock and gave us a hard fight.   Three of our men were killed outright and several were wounded.   We must have made it hard for the whites, for they did not try to follow us.   Several of our horses were killed and some wounded, but we managed to keep the herd together and made our escape. That night we passed a party of Rangers or minute men.   They had left an old negro to guard the horses.   We sent an arrow through his heart, and got away with all of their horses, and hurried away from there before reinforcements could come.

Riding in a run, night and day, never stopping to eat or to sleep until we were away up in the open country, we went back to camp, only to find it deserted. Signs left on the ground there told us that a battle had taken place in which some Tonkaways with whites had been in a measure successful; that the tribe had gone to the sand hills, followed by the Tonkaways and the soldiers, and warned us to be cautious for our enemies would probably be between us and the tribe.

From this camp to the next watering place was at least one hundred miles, so we filled up some cow paunches with water and hung them on our pack horses and set out over this dry country, but fortunately it rained the next day.

Late the next day we came in sight of a camp near a hole of water, so we went away around and our spies made an investigation and reported that only a few men were there with a good herd of horses, and we decided to get those horses, too. So after dark we sent one of the warriors on with the horses we already had and we remained there to see what we could do. We rode up to the horses and found three men guarding them. When we fired on them they took to their heels, while the horses stampeded. Just at this time the soldiers in camp opened fire, and it seemed that there must have been several hundred of them. We fired a few shots into the camp and then ran to round up the horses and start them running in the direction we wanted them to go. We succeeded in getting about forty fine ponies, fresh and rested, so we turned our tired mounts into the herd and rode new ones.

There had been so much shooting and yelling that the Indian who guarded our horse herd thought he was followed and rode off and left us. We came in sight of him and spurred on our fresh horses, but he hurried on, keeping a respectful distance ahead. We raced with him for many miles before he discovered that we were not soldiers, but he had not lost a horse. We put the herds together and we twelve had nearly a hundred good horses and our enemies were practically afoot.

In three or four days we overtook the squaws and children with the camp equipage, and as soon as they learned that several of the warriors with our party had been killed they set up a wailing and began gashing themselves with knives. We lost three braves on this raid, and when we got back to the tribe we had no war dance.

CHAPTER XXX

CANNIBALISM OF THE TONKAWAYS

We knew we could not remain there long, for the whites would hunt us down, and we believed that for every one we killed seven would come to take his place. So we expected the soldiers to be reinforced to follow us. We sent out scouts to find other bands of Comanches and ask them to come and join us, as we moved toward the Mexican border. About seventy-five warriors came to us. We were in no particular hurry, for we reasoned that the soldiers would have to send to the fort to get reinforcements and mounts, so we killed buffalo and traveled leisurely along, occasionally killing a buffalo hunter.

One day three warriors came rushing into camp almost exhausted and told us that they with three other warriors had been surrounded and overpowered by about thirty Tonkaways who were well armed and equipped, and in the fight the three had managed to escape to bring us word of the attack. We had more than three times that number, so we mounted and rode out to meet them. After riding about three hours we located them in camp, having a feast.

The Comanches and Tonkaways had been at war

a long time, and the Tonkaways had been nearly exterminated. The hatred the Tonkaway had for the Comanche was fierce, for they blamed the Comanche for all of their misfortunes and eventually made a treaty with the white people and combined with them to exterminate the Comanche, acting as scouts and trailers and warriors for the whites.

When we found those Tonkaways in camp our chief gave a war-whoop and we all joined in one continual yell as we charged that camp. They fled at the onslaught and several of them were killed. We took possession of the camp, and what do you suppose we found on that fire, roasting? One of the legs of a Comanche! A warrior of our tribe! Our chief gave the cry for vengeance, and we all joined in the chorus. We immediately gave chase. No martial music fascinated our little band and urged us to victory. But one look at those stern faces and drawn muscles would have shown that they meant to utterly annihilate their enemy. The Tonkaways had collected in a ravine and were prepared to receive our charge with a deadly fire, which for a moment checked our onrush; down would come a horse, over would tumble the rider, but on, on, we came, in our frenzy. At first I was terrified, and it seemed like I could not face death that way, but I was in the front rank and my comrades in the rear pressed me onward. Then I caught the spirit of vengeance. I became enraged, spurred on my steed and fought courageously. One of the Tonkaways rode out of the ravine to challenge a single combat. A Comanche made a dash at him, but fell mortally wounded. Another went and received a death blow. It seemed like human blood had made the Tonkaway bold, and somehow our shields would not ward off his bullets, but the third warrior to advance got him. At this single combat, by seemingly general consent, a cessation took place and at this recess every warrior loaded his gun and prepared for eventualities. The combat between the two warriors was of but short duration, and when the Tonkaway brave fell there went up a yell from both sides, exultant from us, a yell of rage from the Tonkaways, and in a very few seconds we were in a hand-to-hand conflict with the Tonkaways, and they were soon vanquished. Those cannibals fought bravely, and eight of our men lay dying on the battlefield, while forty or fifty were more or less desperately wounded. But our work was not finished.

A great many of the dying enemy were gasping for water, but we heeded not their pleadings. We scalped them, amputated their arms, cut off their legs, cut out their tongues, and threw their mangled bodies and limbs upon their own campfire, put on more brushwood and piled the living, dying and dead Tonkaways on the fire. Some of them were able to flinch and work as a worm, and some were able to speak and plead for mercy. We piled them up, put on more wood, and danced around in great glee as we saw the grease and blood run from their bodies, and were delighted to see them swell up and hear the hide pop as it would burst in the fire.

Some of the enemy may have escaped, but we never saw any signs of them. We had twenty-eight scalps, thirty-five split-eared horses, thirty long-range guns, some saddles, a number of blankets, many bows and arrows, besides a great quantity of ammunition and other trophies as a reward for our vengeance, which in some respects partly satisfied our blood-thirsty band.

The reason so many of our men were killed and wounded was because the Tonkaways had the advantage of position and in equipment, and our men were so enraged at the sight of our roasted companion, that we became reckless and did not use our shields properly. I had four spikes and one lead mark on my shield. If a shield is in motion when a ball strikes it the bullet will glance every time.

CANNIBALISM OF THE TONKAWAYS

We returned to camp with our wounded and dead, and also our scalps and other booty. There we found a sad spectacle. Such weeping, moaning, wailing, hair-pulling and gash-cutting. Those squaws cut gashes in their faces and on their bodies and limbs which took months to heal. Besides, those squaws kept the places raw and the wound irritated in order to make their fancied reward greater in the hereafter. There is nothing pleasant nor amusing about a funeral dance, such as we had when we came back from that fight with the Tonkaways.

It was three months before all of our wounded recovered and we could go on another raid. We drifted north, and another band, who had just run away from Fort Sill, joined us, and others came in from different quarters until we became about three hundred strong. We hunted for a while, replenished our stock of buffalo robes, moccasins, wigwams, and other necessities. The women did all of the work, except making bows, arrows, tomahawks and pipes. We robbed several buffalo hunters' camps, leaving the owners destitute and afoot out there on the plains hundreds of miles from home to die of thirst and starvation.

CHAPTER XXXI

QUANAH PARKER

Much has been said and written about Quanah Parker, who became a great Comanche chief. Quanah was the son of Cynthia Ann Parker, a white girl who was captured at Parker's Fort in 1835, and retaken some twenty-eight years later when the Rangers under Sul Ross had a big fight with the Comanches on Pease River, in which it has been reported that Peta Nocona was killed. But Indians who told me of this fight claimed that Peta Nocona was not killed in this engagement, but was killed or died some years later. One old Indian of the Comanche tribe told me in strict confidence that Quanah was not Peta Nocona's son, but was the son of Yotavo, a Mexican, who had been taken captive when he was a small boy and raised among the Indians. This Indian told me that Cynthia Ann Parker had been the squaw of this Mexican, but that Peta Nocona took her away from him while Quanah was a very small child, and raised the boy as his own. I do not believe this, for I knew this old Indian was opposed to Quanah becoming a chief, and I think he tried to discredit him in this way. I have talked to other Indians in regard to the matter, and they assured me that Quanah was the son of Peta Nocona and Cynthia Ann Parker.

Quanah Parker became a great man among the Indians, and was foremost in bringing about peace between the white people and the Indians. It was due to his persuasion that I was induced to come in to the reservation and submit to being restored to my people, after all of my band had surrendered, and he greatly aided me in securing an allotment and headright from the government. I was put down as one of Quanah Parker's boys.

Quanah (fragrant) was, as stated above, the son of Nocona or Nokoni (wanderer), who was the leader of the Kwahadi band, said to be the most hostile portion of the Comanche tribe. Quanah was born about 1845, and grew up with the tribe. After the death of his father he rapidly rose to command- ing influence. His band refused to enter into the Medicine Lodge treaty of 1867, by which the Co- manche, Kiowa, Apache, Cheyenne, and Arapahoe tribes were assigned to reservations, and continued to raid and kill and pillage until 1874, when, in con- sequence of an organized company of white buffalo hunters, Quanah himself mustered the warriors of the Comanche and Cheyenne, with about half the Kiowa and some portion of the other two tribes, for resistance. In June, 1874, an attack led by Quanah in person at the head of about 700 confederate warriors, was launched against some buffalo hunters who were strongly entrenched in a fort known as Adobe Walls, on the South Canadian in the Texas Panhandle. The fight lasted all day and Quanah and his forces were compelled to retire with considerable loss.

The Indians were constant in their hostile movements until the next year, when, being hard pressed by troops under General McKenzie, most of them surrendered. Quanah, however, kept his band out upon the plains for two years longer, when he also surrendered. With keen foresight he recognized the inevitable, that the Indian had to give away before the superior white man, so he set about to make the best of the new conditions and persuade his people to do likewise. Being still young and with the inherited intelligence of his white ancestry, he quickly adapted himself so well to the white man's ways as to become a most efficient factor in leading his people up to civilization. Through his influence the confederated tribes adopted the policy of leasing the surplus pasture lands, by which a large annual income was added to their revenues. He encouraged education, house building and agriculture, and discouraged dissipation and savage extravagance, while holding strictly to his native beliefs and ceremonies. Polygamy being customary in his tribe, he had several wives and a large number of children, all of whom have received a school education, and some of his daughters have married white men. For many years before his death he was the most prominent and influential figure among the three confederated tribes in all leases, treaty negotiations, and other public business with the government, and in this capacity he made repeated visits to Washington, besides having traveled extensively in other parts of the country.

Quanah died February 22, 1912, at his home near Cache, Oklahoma, at the age of sixty-seven years.

CHAPTER XXXII

THE STORY OF A FIGHT

Away up on the plains a large party of our warriors under Quanah Parker (I was not along, though) tackled a party of buffalo hunters, who were making their headquarters in an old adobe enclosure, which had stood there for ages. The Indians could not tell who had put up this old adobe wall, nor how long it had been there. But with the coming of the hundreds of buffalo hunters to the plains, the Indians realized that the game would all be slaughtered and their means of subsistence would be cut off. Naturally, with their hatred of the white man, this encroachment upon their hunting grounds furnished plenty of excuse for declaring war upon the hunters, so when it became known that the old adobe quarters were occupied, steps were at once taken to drive out the palefaces. Accordingly, Quanah mustered his Comanches, some Kiowas and Cheyennes, and attacked the hunters. As stated above, I did not participate in this fight, as I was away on a raid to the south at the time, but I heard about it when I returned from several of the Indians who were engaged in the struggle. Many of our tribe were killed and many wounded by the long-range buffalo guns of the hunters.

THE STORY OF A FIGHT

Quanah himself was wounded, and very severely. There was a negro with the Comanches, a former soldier, who had deserted and came to the Indians, and he had a bugle with which the Indians were drilled to fight something after the fashion of the white men. This negro was killed in the fight, as was also one of the big medicine men of the tribe. I do not know how many of the buffalo hunters were killed, but there were several caught away from the adobe inclosure and killed at the first onset. Our men overtook them near the house, if it may be called a house, and had a hand-to-hand conflict, near some wagons, but several of the hunters gained an entrance to the fort. As the door swung open and one hunter entered, an arrow pierced his heart and he died on the threshold, just as another man pulled him inside. The white men poured a deadly fire from port-holes in the walls, but the Indians kept charging, and even tried to break down the door, but without success. The fight lasted all day, and late that evening the Comanches were so badly disconcerted that they decided to withdraw, so they went away out from the fort, out of gunshot as they thought, and were holding a council trying to devise some means of rescuing their dead that had been left on the battlefield. Suddenly and without any apparent cause one of the warriors tumbled over dead.   He was examined and it was found that a ball had gone through his skull. The wind was blowing, and the buffalo hunter's gun was so long-ranged that the report was not heard, but the effect was quite visible.   That decided the Indians, so they left their dead and went away to get out of reach of such deadly weapons. The Indians told me about this fight, and I think it must have been what was afterwards known as the Adobe Walls fight.

CHAPTER XXXIII

RUNS THROUGH A CAMP OF PALEFACES

At the time of the fight mentioned in the preceding chapter about twelve of the Comanches, including myself, went down near Fort Concho on a raid. There, one Indian, Esatema, and I, both of us being afoot, were left behind by the other Indians, who were mounted. We went on and came near a small town, perhaps it was Paint Rock, I do not know, and we discovered a tent, and near the tent a horse was staked. I had a long-range gun, and I told Esatema that if he would sneak up and steal the horse I would hold the gun in readiness and shoot the first white man that appeared, but he would not do it. He said we were there afoot, and he wanted a horse to ride, but if we killed a white man then we would have but little chance to get out of the country. Then I asked him if he would take the gun and shoot any white man who appeared if I would go and get the horse, and he promised to do so. I sneaked around and approached the horse, which kept snorting and cutting capers. When I got hold of the stake rope I cut it, and led the horse away. Esatema and I were able to ride off without being molested.

From there we went east, and late that evening

,we found a camp near which was a large bunch of horses. One of the horses had a large bell on. When the campers went to sleep that night Esatema and I shot arrows into the horse that wore the bell and killed him to keep him from running and awakening the campers. Then we silently rounded up the other horses, about twenty-five, and started in a dead run for our headquarters away up on the plains. We traveled for three days without seeing anyone or being bothered. We were going through a pass in the mountains, possibly it was Buffalo Gap, and ran right into a camp of white men before we saw them. Realizing that we had to act promptly we put our herd into a run and went through that camp yelling and shooting. It was just at daylight, and the sleeping men arose as one man and made a break for the brush, not taking time to get their guns. As we went through we picked up two of their horses and carried them along, but we did not tarry to find out how many men were in the camp, and as they did not follow us we made a safe get-away. We soon struck the buffalo trails, which insured obliteration of our herd trail, and reached our village with a good bunch of horses. The other ten Indians who had gone out with us came back empty-handed.

Before getting back to the village Esatema and

I killed a deer for meat, which we had not eaten
for some time. We had lost our only knife and
could not skin the deer, so we were quite perplexed
as to how we could remove its hide. Finally we
got hold of it with our teeth and pulled the hide off.
As we had no way to cut up the venison we threw
the carcass on the fire and roasted it whole.

We stayed around the village some time, preparing to make a move to a safer region. The defeat
of the big band of warriors at the adobe fort had
somewhat disheartened us, for we felt that the
white buffalo hunters were going to come in such
numbers that the Indians would have no more hunting ground on the plains. Our men were getting
scarcer every day, war parties and raiders would
go out and never return. We held a great council,
in which other tribes participated, and pledged ourselves to kill all of the whites as they came into our
territory; kill them as they destroyed our game;
kill them as they slew our warriors; kill them as
they killed our squaws and children; to follow them
and kill them so long as any of us remained, and
on the break-up of the council we had a big war
dance.

We robbed the camps of buffalo hunters and
killed them as we found them. We moved north
and we found the plains were literally alive with

buffalo hunters. We came back across the plains still fighting those pesky hunters. These were exciting times, for scarcely a day passed without a skirmish or a fight, and it looked like our warriors would all soon be killed out. Down near the southeast edge of the plains we would leave our women and children and old men and go on a raid. Starting out on a raid we would divide our party as usual, but into smaller numbers, as the country was getting so thickly settled and the Rangers so numerous and bold, we did not dare risk a large party out together. I had Esatema as a companion, and he was a brave, daring fellow, very cautious, and always used good judgment. We stole many horses, and left many white men dead or wounded, scalped and lacerated, dodged the Rangers, slipped back and stampeded their horses while they were burying their dead comrades, and left many of the brave palefaces afoot.

Marco, a Mexican captive, and I went on a raid down east, and on a little stream we found some men camping. We went back a short distance and held a consultation and decided to attack them, so we loaded our guns and started for their camp, whooping and yelling, and just as we got even with the camp we shot into their campfire. There were four men and they scattered. Their horses stampeded, but of course we could not stop there long. We went around the horses, captured nine of them, and pulled for home.

On another raid twelve of us came down east and met a four-horse stage near Kickapoo Springs. Several men were with the stage so we had a running fight for several miles, but we had to draw off and let that stage go on its way. We came on and met five palefaces and had a fight with them. They hid behind trees and fought us after our own manner of fighting. These men took aim when they shot and our shields were all that saved some of us. The battle was a stand-off and none of us were killed, but those fellows shot too close for our comfort. I do not know how they fared in the fight, for we withdrew and they never followed.

Down near Smoothing Iron Mountain we took twenty-five horses, tore down some fences and left things like we believed the Great Spirit intended them to be, free and open. The Indians believed that if the Great Spirit had wanted the country enclosed He would have fenced it. We came back by House Mountain and stole some horses and one old mule and struck a bee-line for the plains, for the Rangers were after us. They overtook us and fought us, captured all of our loose horses, and we scattered, drifting west and coming together near Beaver Lake. The chief said that the Great Spirit had told him that if we would follow the Rangers and surprise them that we would gain an easy victory.

We located the Rangers in camp near a water hole, and taking a good survey of the ground, we cautiously approached their camp, but the Rangers were not easily taken by surprise, for when we were within about fifty yards of them they fired on us, wounded one warrior and killed a horse. They were camped around a big live oak tree. We charged them, but they made us purchase with blood every foot of ground we gained. While the fight was raging two of our warriors succeeded in stampeding their (our) horses and when they got them safely away we quit the battle and went to them, and made our get-away. Several of our warriors were severely wounded.

We returned to the plains, where we constantly waged war on the buffalo hunters. We had to be on the alert, for hardly a day passed but what we saw soldiers or signs of them, and they seemed bent on putting us on the reservation.

CHAPTER XXXIV

KILLING A BUFFALO HUNTER

The plains were being thoroughly combed by the buffalo hunters, who were killing buffalo for their hides. We would often see great wagon loads of hides being hauled away, and would find the carcasses of thousands of slaughtered buffalo. It made us desperate to see this wanton slaughter of our food supply.

One day quite a party of us came upon a buffalo hunter away from his camp killing buffalo. He had killed several of them, and about this time we saw two men in a wagon start out from the camp to go to him, presumably to skin the buffaloes that lay dead upon the ground. We circled around this lone hunter and soon killed and scalped him and then took after the two who were coming from the camp. They saw us about that time and turned their team around and whipped into a run, heading for a little brushy ravine some distance away, and when they reached it they plunged over the steep bank, abandoned the wagon and team and took to the brush. We did not find them, and they got away safely. We went to the hunters' camp and destroyed everything we found there which we did not want to take away. We then went back to the

171

body of the hunter we had killed and took two scalp locks from his head, cut a gash in each temple and thrust a sharp stick through his stomach. One of the warriors took the hunter's gun and claimed it for his own. It was the longest range gun I ever saw, and every Indian wanted it, but it sure brought bad luck to the Indian who secured it. After we left there the buffalo hunters took our trail and followed us for a long time. Finally we had a fight with them and the Indian who had the big gun was killed. Another Indian got the gun and claimed it for his own. He, too, was killed. Then it passed into the possession of the chief's son, and he fell with it in his hands. Then an Indian known as Five Feathers used it for a long time, when he, too, was killed. The medicine man said the gun had an evil spirit and advised us to throw it away or hide it where the white men could never find it. So we buried the big gun and the two scalp-locks taken from the head of the buffalo hunter in the sand hills.

CHAPTER XXXV

I GET SHOT IN THE LEG

I have often been asked if I was ever wounded while I was with the Indians. I carry several wound scars which I received in battle. One of the scars is from a bullet through the shoulder, and another is a scar made by a bullet from a buffalo gun, which passed through the calf of my right leg, and laid me up for quite a while. I received this wound in a fight with white men who attacked our camp just after daylight one morning, and at a time when we least expected to be attacked. There was a big bunch of the whites, and for a time it looked as if they would whip us. As soon as the fight started, the squaws mounted and got our horses out of the camp to prevent them from falling into the hands of the white men. We took refuge under a hillside and held the enemy, who were in the open, at bay for several hours, when they finally retreated.

When the bullet struck me in the leg I guess I was too excited to feel it, and I went right on fighting. But after a while the wound began to pain me considerably and I had to lay down. One Indian was knocked down by a bullet, and we thought he was killed, but it proved to be only a scalp wound. We were so well concealed under that hill that not an Indian was killed, but I think the enemy lost several men. I was using a long-range buffalo gun at the time, and I think I hit the mark with it several times. The whites withdrew and we gathered up our squaws and children and horses and moved away from there.

One amusing thing to the Indians happened in this fight which I was about to forget to relate. We captured a fat negro who was with the attacking party, and brought him into camp. He was almost scared to death, and fell on his knees to beg for his life. The chief had him stripped and then made him put on an Indian's garb, and a war bonnet was tied upon his head so securely that he could not get it off. Then the Indians made signs to him to run back to his white friends. He understood the signs and lit out, but when the white men saw him coming they thought he was an Indian and shot him full of holes. He fell before he reached his friends.

After we gathered our horses and women we traveled across the plains and met the Apaches. They asked me to rejoin them, but I would not, and while I was in their camp you can be assured that I kept my eyes open and was on the alert for any sign of treachery or attack upon me. One old Apache watched me closely, and I was certain he would make some attempt to avenge the killing of the medicine man whom I slew before I went into exile, but I gave him no opportunity to kill me. The Comanches were watchful, too, and when they discovered what they took to be a plot against me, they became angered at the Apaches, who went on, leaving us there. The Comanches had taken an oath to protect me, and they did. The Apaches were afraid of being attacked that night, so they went clear away.

That is the last and only time I came in contact with that tribe after I left them and went to the Comanches. I have met some members of the tribe on reservations in Oklahoma in later years, and talked with them, but they did not always belong to the band which had sworn to get me. Old Chiwat, who is still living at Indiahoma, Oklahoma, and now nearly one hundred years old, is an Apache, and helped to capture me. He has remained my life-long friend. Chiwat is a pretty good old Indian. After the tribe was placed on the reservation he became a scout for the government and rendered good service in trailing marauding bands of runaway tribes.

CHAPTER XXXVI

I CATCH AN ARROW IN THE KNEE

In these days of modern ways people get shot just about as they got shot in olden times, and there is usually a woman at the bottom of the trouble. And a beautiful Indian maiden was the cause of me catching an arrow in my knee, some time after I joined the Comanches. Topay was her name, and for her I had a passing fancy. It soon passed. Her father did not take well to our courtship; in fact, he told me to stay away from her and let her alone, but I would not. One night, by agreement, I went into her tepee after the parents had "retired," and we thought the father was sound asleep. Now, this need not shock the modesty of those who may read this, for with the Indian all nature took its course and we had none of those "petting parties" now in vogue. I had told my sweetheart about the threats her father had made and asked her if we should not be more cautious, but she said he would not hurt me, although he might try to scare me. I was whispering sweet words of love to her and enjoying Elysian bliss here on earth when suddenly I felt a rough kick, and I needed not a second hint for I knew it was the toe of the girl's father's moccasin. Out I went, leaving a pretty considerable hole in the tent. The old man filled up the door and I was compelled to go out under the bottom of the tepee. I went around the tent one way and he came around the other, and as we met he let fly an arrow which pierced me in the knee. I sank to the ground, unable to walk. The wound was very painful and I was lame from it for a long time. The girl came to me and took her place by my side, and rebuked her father for treating me in such a brutal manner. The old man weakened, forgave us for sparking on the sly, pulled out the arrow, and showed his regrets in many ways, even to the extent of offering to let me take the girl for my squaw if I would give him two ponies. But I "shied off," and have been afraid of women ever since.

When an Indian chose a wife, in both the Apache and Comanche tribes, he had to purchase the girl from her parents with horses. A brave would fall in love with a maiden and he would approach her father and make his wants known by offering him a certain number of horses for the girl, and if his proposition was accepted he would deliver the horses, take the girl and conduct her to his tepee. There was no religious ceremony, no demonstration, no incantations, or anything else to make the marriage impressive or of more than passing interest.

The buck had procured the squaw, and the squaw had found a master. Sometimes the father of the girl would make the first advances by offering his daughter to some warrior for a certain number of horses, in which event it was usually the prospective son-in-law's privilege to drive a good bargain.

Children were often born to Apache squaws who were with raiding parties. The Indians would permit their squaws to go with them on their raids, and if it so happened that a child was born the squaw would be left to take care of herself as best she could, or if another squaw was in the party and chose to remain with her sister in distress, she was allowed to do so. Within a reasonable time the squaw and her papoose would come into camp and there would be rejoicing if the papoose happened to be a male child, because that meant a future warrior. But if it happened to be a female, no notice would be taken of the new arrival. I have known squaws to give birth to a child, abandon it immediately and proceed on with the party, with no apparent injury. I knew one squaw of the Apaches who gave birth to twins, and she became so angry because there were two children instead of one that she stamped her offspring to death and left their little bodies for the vultures to devour.

Comanche women were kinder to their children,

and the births usually occurred in the villages. A woman in delicate health was not allowed to accompany her warrior on a raid, but had to remain in camp until the looked-for event happened. They carefully nourished the new-born babe and bestowed upon their children, male and female, that motherly affection that was the child's due. What we would now term illegitimate children were rare among the Indians. There was virtue among the Indians and it was rigidly maintained. Of course there were times when a married woman "went wrong," in which case her nose was cut off, but it was seldom that an unmarried girl departed from the paths of decency and gave birth to a child.

CHAPTER XXXVII

WE OUTRAN THE DOGS

One day two Indians, Watsacatova and Esatema, and I were down in the outskirts of civilization on a raid for horses. We were afoot, but had a pack mule along to carry our equipment, and each took turn about riding this mule. We were out on the prairie not far from a broken country, and not a great ways off was a stream. We discovered some white people camped on the stream. Northeast of the camp we saw a dense thicket, so we decided to conceal our pack mule in that thicket and make a raid on that camp. To reach that thicket we had to cross an open country in front of the campers, but fortunately there was a little ravine which we followed and were on our way to the thicket when suddenly a wagon came rattling right up to us. Watsacatova and Esatema had good needle guns and an abundance of ammunition, while I had a fine pistol and at least one hundred cartridges, besides our bows and arrows. This wagon contained three white men and they were leading a saddled horse behind the vehicle. The sudden appearance of the white men caused us to act quickly, and we fired a volley at them. All three men left the wagon, one man mounted the saddle horse and lit out for

180

the camp. For a moment the other two men seemed dazed, then they climbed back into the wagon and whipped the horses into a run and made for camp. Within a short time we saw about a dozen armed men coming toward us with several bloodhounds, so we beat it from there. Esatema was young and agile, so he outsped us. Watsacatova was big and fat, but he understood the situation and kept quite a distance ahead of me. We leaped over the ground, ahead of those hounds until we had covered fully six miles, sometimes slackening our pace until the dogs almost reached us, when we seemed to get new inspiration to speed. Watsacatova began to get out of breath, or rather get too much on hand, and I overtook him at a critical moment, when it seemed that the dogs had also received some of that inspiration we had been getting. He said to me: "Don't leave me. Let us stop and fight. I can't run any further." I noticed that he would have left me at first if he could, so I ran by him. Just then the sound of horses' hoofs was right at us, but fortune was in our favor, for right before us was a great bluff and beyond was a mighty yawning deep. We dreaded not the leap from that bluff, but the bullets of our white pursuers was what we were afraid of. Down that bluff we rolled, like a coon descending a tree, encountering vines and bushes. In rolling down Watsacatova's long dangling hair, done up in cow-tail fashion, became entangled in some bushes and in his hasty extrication the queue was jerked out, leaving a bloody scalp. We reached the bottom scratched, torn and bruised, but still able to run. The dogs followed us down the precipice, but the horsemen had to go around. The dogs were not keen to overtake us when their masters were not near. I do not know why, but I suppose they had a presentiment that it was very well to chase their retreating foes, but it was not well to catch them. We found a river and plunged in, but instead of going straight across we floated downstream. The dogs lost our trail and we made good our escape. We still had our guns, but our other possessions were stored away on the mule, hidden in the thicket near the white men's camp.

A fellow does not know how far he can run until he has the hope of life in flight and the knowledge of death in being overtaken. That acts as a goad to urge him on when all other incentives fail.

We checked our pace, stopped, found a bee-cave, took some honey, mixed it with a little water, killed a beef, made some sauce out of the water, honey and tallow, and spread it over the meat after it had been well roasted, and we had a feast. We cut the hide of the yearling and made some lariats and went on further and stole three horses. The next night we found ourselves in the vicinity of a small town, and there we stole a bunch of horses and made a run for our headquarters.

The fate of the pack mule is still shrouded in mystery, and for all I know he may be standing there tied in that thicket yet. We never went back to see about him, for we were many miles away from him when we got rid of those dogs.

How Watsacatova's squaw did laugh when she saw her master's bald head! He looked as if he had been scalped, and the other Indians derided him for losing his top-knot by running so fast. His hair never grew back, and he carried a bald spot on the top of his head to his grave.

One time, while I was with the Comanches, a band of warriors, including several Kiowas, were out on the Pecos and we discovered a large herd of cattle being driven by ten or twelve cowboys. We stampeded the herd and drove off the cattle. The cowboys at first put up a stiff fight, and then ran. Two of the cowboys were killed in the scrap, but we outnumbered them two to one, and if they had not sought refuge in tall running we would have killed all of them. We drove the cattle away out on the plains to our camp, and killed some of them, the others were turned loose on the prairie and for a long time we would go out and slaughter them as we needed meat.   This fight took place near what is known as the Pontoon Crossing on the Pecos, and years later I met a man who knew all about that fight, knew the two cowboys who were killed, and said they were buried there on the Pecos River. He may have told me their names, but if he did I have forgotten them.   So many incidents like that happened during my wild life that I never tried to remember the details.

CHUCKO, COMANCHE CHIEF
Friend and companion, now lives at Cache, Okla.

CHAPTER XXXVIII

SOLDIERS KILL OUR WOMEN

We were all camped down near the southern border of the plains and a large party of us went down on the San Saba and Llano Rivers and got a big lot of horses. Those early settlers were very kind to raise horses for us, for it saved us a lot of trouble. As we were leaving that region our scouts reported that we were being followed by the Rangers, so we hurried along and outran them. When we reached our camp we found it had been attacked by a body of soldiers and some Tonkaway Indians, and a number of our women were among the slain. Several women and children were made captives and had been taken to Fort Griffin. When the attack was made on the camp most of the squaws ran away and hid, but five of them were killed while escaping. We arrived the next day after the fight and found the dead bodies scattered about. I remember finding the body of Batsena, a very brave warrior, lying mutilated and scalped, and alongside of him was the horribly mangled remains of his daughter, Nooki, a beautiful Indian maiden, who had been disemboweled and scalped. The bodies presented a revolting sight. Nearby lay a lot of empty Spencer carbine cartridge shells, telling mutely of the heroic fight old Batsena had put up in defense of his own. His Spencer rifle was gone, of course, but I have no doubt that it worked deadly execution before it was taken. Other bodies were mutilated, too, which showed the hand of the Tonkaway in the bloody battle.

We soon found our scattered women and children and old men, and heard the sad details of the attack, and our rage knew no bounds. Five of our women and several children were captives in the hands of the soldiers. In our council we swore to take ten captive white women and twice as many white children, and to avenge the death of our squaws, especially Nooki; we vowed to kill a white woman for each year of her age (she was about 18 years old), and that we would disembowel every one we killed. Some of the warriors were for going back into the settlements at once and starting in on our revenge, but we were so badly demoralized that we had to get our forces together and move to another part of the country before seeking vengeance.

We went far up on the plains, and Quanah Parker and four other Indians came to us and urged us to go on the reservation, saying that the Indians' wild life was over. Quanah told us that it was useless for us to fight longer, for the white people would kill all of us if we kept on fighting, but that if we went on the reservation the Great White Father at Washington would feed us, and give us homes, and we would in time become like the white men, with lots of good horses and cattle, and pretty things to wear. He said the white men had us completely surrounded; that they would come in on us from every side, and we had better give up. Some of the braves wanted to go to the reservation at Fort Sill, and some did not want to go, so there was much disputing and arguing. Quanah remained with us about four days, promising us that if we would go to Fort Sill we would not be punished or hurt in any way, and that all would be well with us. Finally our band agreed to go in, and when Quanah started we went along with him.

There were several of us who went reluctantly, myself, Hishorty, Cotopah, Esatema, and Watsacatova. We started on and Quanah sent scouts ahead to notify the soldiers at Fort Sill that we were coming in, and to give us all protection. In a few days we began to meet white people everywhere, but as Quanah could speak English we got along all right.

We were within about fifteen miles of Fort Sill when I saw a cloud of dust and heard the soldiers coming to meet us. I was riding a black mare and a pretty swift animal, so I turned and rode for life

187

back toward the Wichita Mountains. Quanah took after me and ran me for three or four miles before he caught me. He told me there was no need to be afraid, that I would not be hurt. I would not agree to go with him; then he told me to go to his camp, and gave me directions how to get there. When he got back to the crowd the soldiers were there and had my comrades surrounded. All were disarmed and were taken on to Fort Sill, where they were placed in a stockade and kept prisoners for some time. I followed Quanah's instructions and found his camp without being seen by the soldiers. My comrades were made to work around the post and to do farm work, with which they were not familiar. I stayed with Quanah and herded his horses for him, hunted occasionally, and soon became somewhat reconciled to my situation.

After they had been at Fort Sill for a while two of our Indians, Esatema and Eschito, who had to stand guard and watch cattle, allowed some of the cattle to get away. They were punished for this, and had to chop wood. This so exasperated them that they planned to escape, and when one of the Indians asked their guard for some tobacco, the other knocked him in the head with an axe. He fell, and they secured his gun and ammunition and ran away.

CHAPTER XXXIX

ATTEMPT TO ASSASSINATE ME

I had not been with Quanah Parker very long before I discovered that there were a good many Apaches in that region, who had been brought under control of the government, and among them were some of my old tribe in whose breasts still lurked the spirit of revenge. That they would make some kind of an attempt to kill me I had no doubt, so I was on the alert. One night I was riding along by myself, returning from taking a bunch of horses out to grass, when suddenly several shots were fired at me. It was very dark, but I saw the flashes of the gun and knew where the shots came from. I fell off of my horse and lay perfectly still. They fired again, and I raised up and emptied my pistol at the cowards. In a few seconds I heard somebody groaning. I then ran to Quanah's and on the way I passed a big black stump. I did not see this stump until I was right near it, and thinking it was a man I shot at it as I went by. When I reported the matter to Quanah he called up his men and found five were missing. Search was made and they were soon found, carrying a wounded Indian. They had all kinds of excuses, the main one being that they just wanted to scare me.

Some cowardly Apaches had hired these Indians to kill me. They had an Apache horse and that was what gave them away. They finally acknowledged the whole plot.

Some time after this I got very sick and thought for a while I was going to die. Yellow Wolf was a big medicine man and lived with Quanah Parker. He boiled a lot of herbs and gave me a villainous concoction to drink, and kept me wrapped in poultices, and nursed me carefully until I recovered. Poor old Yellow Wolf. He died some years ago from asphyxiation while he and Quanah Parker were stopping at a hotel in Fort Worth. They blew out the gas. Next morning Yellow Wolf was found dead and Quanah Parker was almost dead.

One day, after my convalescence, Quanah wanted me to go to the post with him. We went there and the soldiers surrounded me and called me "Charlie Ross," and as long as I was there I was called that name. They wanted to keep me at the post, and the commanding officer told Quanah my people were still living and I should be sent to them. Quanah told me my mother and folks were still alive, and asked me if I wanted to go to them. I told him no; that the Indians were my people, and I would not go with the whites. Quanah told me he would leave me there at the post with the soldiers, and I became very angry with him, telling him that he was doing me wrong to bring me there and leave me with those soldiers. They took me to talk to a Comanche interpreter named Jones, who said I would have to go to my people, and when I told him I would never consent to go he said they would take me anyhow. At this remark I pulled my bow, fitted an arrow, and Colonel Jones made haste to get out of the danger zone. Quanah stopped me and told me that he would see that they did not take me, for he was going back to his wigwam with me. I turned and was going to kill Jones anyhow, but he was gone.

I went back home with Quanah and we talked over the matter a great deal, and finally I was persuaded to give up. I went to the post and stayed a day. The soldiers were good to me, but I was not satisfied. They put me across the creek with my former comrades and I lay around. The soldiers furnished us rations and ammunition, but we yearned for freedom.

One Indian proposed to me that we steal a squaw apiece and run away. I went and talked to a girl and she consented to go. We were to meet that night. My comrade stole another Indian's squaw, got two good horses and made good his escape. My girl was true to her promise, stole everything she

191

could carry and waited for me until nearly daylight. I started and when I was nearly to where she was waiting the soldiers discovered me and gave chase. I ran off of a bluff and fell into the creek and came near freezing, and was eventually driven back to camp. So many soldiers watched me that I had no chance to escape.

About this time General McKenzie saw my mother in Fredericksburg and told her about me being at Fort Sill. From the description he gave her of me mother did not think I was her boy.

Adolph Korn, whom I had met once while a Comanche party was visiting the Apaches, had been at home for several years; Rudolph Fischer had been sent home about three months before, and I was the only white boy left with the Indians.

General McKenzie came back to Fort Sill, and they began to talk to me about going home to my people. Quanah Parker told me how to find the way back to his camp, and promised to take care of my horses while I was gone. He said he would be a brother to me, and insisted that if I did not have any people that I should come back and live with him.

CHAPTER XL

MY RESTORATION

I left all of my Indian property with Quanah, and in company with five soldiers and a driver I started to Loyal Valley, in Mason County, Texas, to see my mother. We traveled in an ambulance drawn by four mules, and made about twenty miles the first day. Four days' traveling brought us into a country where there was game, and the soldiers would place a gun in my hands and make signs to me to go out and kill an antelope, and I would always "bring home the bacon." The fifth day one of the soldiers went with me and when we got out of sight of the ambulance, I planned to kill him and run away. But after thinking over the matter I concluded that I had no place to go. So I decided to give that soldier a good scare anyway. I got the drop on him and made signs for him to lay down his gun. He did not want to but I soon convinced him that I was in earnest and he put it on the ground and raised his hands in the air. I pointed toward camp and said, "Vamos!" He understood that and lit out for camp in a hurry. I picked up his gun and went to camp myself. The other soldiers laughed at the one who came in ahead of me for letting an Indian boy take his gun away from him, and they made sport of him throughout the trip.

I played all sorts of pranks on those soldiers. One morning I grabbed up a blanket, waved it over my head two or three times, and gave the Comanche war-whoop, and I want you to know those fellows scattered, and the mules broke loose. They took it all good natured, and seemed to enjoy the fun.

We came to Fort Griffin and the five soldiers got on a big drunk, and all of them were sent to the guardhouse, and a new outfit was selected to escort me. I was allowed to kill game for them, too, and do pretty much as I pleased, but they kept an eye on me all the time. We came to a big water hole and the soldiers caught some big bullfrogs and fried them in lard. But I would not eat them, for it was against the Comanche's rule to eat lard. I would not eat with those soldiers any more. Frogs and swine, both water or mud animals, were too much for me.

The second day after leaving Fort Griffin I jumped off of the wagon and shot an antelope. One of the soldiers brought the little animal in, and as he was climbing into the wagon while it was in motion his foot slipped, the mules jumped and he fell and the wagon ran over his leg, breaking it.

After this we traveled slowly, camped often and

killed game, but gradually we neared the home of my childhood. We passed through Fort Mason and went on to the Llano River to the Simmonsville Crossing. Here we began to meet people who had come out from Loyal Valley to wait for us, word having preceded us that the captive boy was being brought home. When we reached Loyal Valley we drove up and stopped at a place, and the soldiers made signs for me to get out. Quite a crowd of people gathered around, and among them was my mother, but I did not know her. The years of savagery which had passed over my head had erased from my memory all of the recollections of a mother's love and tenderness, and to me in that hour which should have been a crowning event of happiness, my mother was no more than a white squaw. Curiously the crowd examined me, and excitedly talked in a language I could not understand, although it was my native tongue. They looked for marks of identification and found a scar on my arm that was made when I was a little boy. Soon my brother and sister, Willie and Mina, came up, and the dark curtain of oblivion which had been drawn so long, was pulled back and to me there came the recollection of my early childhood. I was restored. I recognized my brother and sister, and remembered them as my playmates in the far distant past. Then somebody kept saying "Herman, Herman," and that name had a familiar sound. It then occurred to me that that was my own name. Slowly but surely the mists began to clear away, and I knew I had found my people. But I was an Indian, and I did not like them because they were palefaces.

CHAPTER XLI

THE TRIUMPH OF A MOTHER'S LOVE

I was five years old when my father, Maurice Lehmann, died; some years later my mother married Philip Buchmier, who died some time in the 90's.

During my captivity my mother never lost hope that some day I would be restored to her. She had talked with Adolph Korn after he was restored to his people and he told her that he had seen me with the Apaches and that I was still alive. So when she received word that there was a captive white boy at Fort Sill she was determined to ascertain if it was me, and have me brought home. The meeting related in the preceding chapter was the realization of her hopes that I was her boy, and her prayers for my restoration were answered. In order to give the full details of this meeting I give below an account which was written by the late John Warren Hunter, who was an intimate friend of our family for many years, he having taught school at Loyal Valley in the early days. This account was published in Hunter's Magazine in 1911:

"Some time in 1878, General McKenzie left Fort Sill and made an inspection of the frontier posts. He passed through Fort Concho, Fort McKavett, thence to San Antonio. At old Fort Mason, which is twenty miles north of Loyal Valley, he spent the night. When his presence in Mason became known friends sent word to Mrs. Buchmier that General McKenzie would pass through Loyal Valley the day following, and that as he was direct from Fort Sill, she would perhaps have an opportunity to learn something of her son.

"Unfortunately Mrs. Buchmier was away when the courier came, but others were immediately dispatched, but before they reached her, General McKenzie and escort had passed Loyal Valley and were well on their way to Fredericksburg, where they expected to spend the following night. When Mrs. Buchmier received word that General McKenzie was expected to pass through Loyal Valley she rode with the speed of a Bedouin to reach home in time to intercept him, but failing in this, she hitched a team of fresh horses to her carriage, and accompanied by her husband, drove like Jehu and came up with the General before he reached Fredericksburg. Of the interview with General McKenzie and its happy results we will allow Mrs. Buchmier to relate her own story."

"Time passed away so slowly. I increased my efforts to learn something of Herman. My faith was thoroughly tested. I heard one day that Gen-

eral McKenzie was coming through Loyal Valley
and I hastened to intercept him, as I thought that
would be a good chance to find out if there were
any more white boys among the Indians that had
come into the reservations and given up. But he
passed down before I could get to see him. I got
my husband to hitch up and carry me to Fredericksburg. We followed on and overtook the General
in his camp three miles this side of Fredericksburg.
I was conducted to his tent and knew him as soon
as I saw him. I told him when Herman was stolen
and as he had just come from the reservation I
thought perhaps he could tell me something of my
boy. He asked me to give him the age and description of my son as near as I could. When I
had done so he said: 'There is one white boy there,
but from the description you give I don't think he
is your son, for he is not that old.' He dropped
his head and studied for a while, and then he said:
'Madam, I'll tell you what we'll do; we'll go on to
Fredericksburg and telegraph the soldiers to bring
him down, and if he is your boy I will be very glad,
but if he should prove not to be your son, I will
have him taken to San Antonio and place him where
he can learn a trade. He has no business with the
Indians.' He telegraphed to the commanding
officer at Fort Sill to send an escort with the white

boy immediately to Loyal Valley, but received the reply that the boy had gone on a buffalo hunt and would not be back for three months. These were the longest three months I ever spent. I could never wait more than two weeks until I would go to the office and telegraph to know if he had returned from the hunt. At last a telegram came, saying he had returned and with the escort would start immediately. Think of my anxiety and joy, mixed with doubt and fear! If he should be my long lost son I would be the happiest mother in the world. I counted the days, and many little things brought up doubts and fears. I trembled at everything; I was wholly unnerved. I inquired of everybody who came from that way if they had seen or heard of soldiers coming, but I obtained no tidings. One morning a man passed soldiers between Loyal Valley and Mason. These soldiers, he said, had charge of the white boy and they sent me word that they were coming and would arrive that night. I walked the floor, only pausing to listen for the sound of their ambulance, but I could hear nothing but the patter of the rain against the window panes. While we were at supper a large crowd came in and said: 'Mrs. Buchmier, we have come to take you out to meet your boy.' Mr. Buchmier objected to my going out in the rain; he said that my going would not hasten things along any. A school teacher who boarded with us said, 'Boys, you go and meet Herman; the night is too disagreeable for Mrs. Buchmier to go out, and no one knows what she would do were she to meet him in the road.' The boys went out three miles, where they found them in camp. They asked the soldiers to hitch up and drive into the Valley that night, and they did so. Meanwhile, the teacher and Mr. Buchmier made me sit down and they were holding me there. Friends had come from far and near to rejoice with me, if it should prove to be my boy. There were three hundred people present. Closer and closer came the sounds of the wheels of the ambulance, while my heart beat faster and faster. Was that ambulance to bring me my boy? It drove up to the door, but they still held me. I tore loose, ran to Herman, threw my arms around his neck and wept. I then led him to the light, and, Great Lord! I thought it was not Herman. Mina came up and said, 'Mamma, it is Herman; don't you see the scar on his hand? That is where I cut him with our little hatchet.' Sure enough, a close examination proved it to be Herman. Imagine the joy, the bliss and happiness that assurance brought me. I shall ever be grateful to General McKenzie for having my boy brought home."

CHAPTER XLI

"Those who witnessed this happy meeting add a number of facts not mentioned by Mother Buchmier. Numbers of them have told me that it was near the noon hour when she received word that the escort would be at Loyal Valley that night. She immediately began preparations for a great feast. She found willing hands among the villagers to aid her. She started runners in every direction to call in friends, far and near; every oven and stove in town was kept hot, baking bread and cakes; beeves and muttons were slaughtered and a pall of smoke ascended from pits of barbecued meats. A slow rain began falling in the evening, but that did not retard preparations for the feast, nor did it lessen the attendance. Everybody loved Mrs. Buchmier; knew how she had prayed, and trusted, and now that the lost son had been found and was nearing home, they hastened to join in the general thanksgiving.

"When the boy arrived and she made sure that he was her son, those present relate that never before had they heard such shouts of praise and thanksgiving to God for His goodness and mercy. The good mother was a devout Methodist, and her righteous soul became full to overflowing and she gave way. There was no dearth of tears of joy that evening; feasting, singing hymns of praise, German and English, prayers of thanksgiving occupied most of the night. All the day following the feast was kept up for those who remained, and those who continued to come. During all this time Herman maintained a haughty indifference akin to Indian stoicism. He had forgotten his mother tongue, and could not speak English. He sought every occasion to shun the company of others, and when assigned to a clean feather bed in which to sleep, he refused, preferring to sleep on the ground with only a blanket for a covering. When the escort left he wanted to return with the soldiers and was with difficulty restrained. One of his brothers became his constant companion, teaching him his forgotten language, and to prevent him from running away. He was given a few horses and cattle in order that a property ownership might serve to render him content to remain. It was a difficult matter to induce him to wear clothing, and oftentimes he would doff the suit furnished him, paint himself, and with leggins, breech-clout and feathers, appear among the hotel guests in all the barbaric panoply of a Comanche warrior.

"A few weeks after his return, a protracted meeting was being held under a brush arbor in Loyal Valley. Herman viewed the proceedings from a respectable distance, and his amazement was extreme.

CHAPTER XLI

He finally concluded the whites were having a rain dance, and one day at the 11 o'clock service, when religious feeling became intense, and singing and shouting was at its height, Herman dashed into the altar with his war club, and engaged in a war dance that had a startling effect. His brothers seized him and led him away, and the service closed without the benediction."

CHAPTER XLII

I BECOME RECONCILED TO CIVILIZATION

My mother was keeping a hotel in Loyal Valley at the time of my return, and had several boarders, some traveling men; all of the family and many of the people of the community gathered around me. Some were laughing, some crying, and all talking. I did not like this kind of a demonstration and made up my mind that I would go back to Quanah Parker. The soldiers told my sister, Mina, how I liked my food, so she fixed it as near to my whim as possible for a civilized person to do. Everyone did all that could be done for me, but I did not like any of them. That night I would not sleep in the house, although they prepared a nice feather bed for me and arranged everything for my comfort. I made a pallet of my own blankets out on the ground, but Willie Lehmann slept with me.

Next day when the soldiers started to go, I was ready to go with them, but they made me understand that they were coming back for me. But no, I was going with them anyhow. They had to slip away from me or I would have gone.

My folks prepared a big feast for me and Mina came to invite me to the table. I pretended not to hear her, but lay on my pallet. I was homesick and was planning then to run away from there. Finally she induced me to go to the table, and just as I was ready to sit down I saw a fine hog ham on the table. I kicked over everything in my reach and made for the door, but they stopped me and motioned for me to come and eat. I pointed to the pork and made them understand that if they would remove that I would eat. It was removed and I sat down and tried to eat, but the food did not suit me and the thought of having to eat with hog-eaters choked me. I wanted my meat roasted, and I didn't care for anything else.

I sat around and smoked cigarettes; one thing I did enjoy was good tobacco. I went down on the creek, made a bow and a great many arrows, and waged war against the hog family. Whenever a shoat came in sight I would kill him, no matter to whom he belonged.

I would saddle up my pony and go out hunting. Somebody gave me a Winchester and my step-father furnished me with cartridges. Willie always went with me to watch me and teach me. I wanted to kill calves, but Willie made signs to me that it was wrong. I insisted that we take all the horses we saw, but Willie would not allow that, so I was mad all of the time; in fact, nothing pleased me.

When I met children I would give a yell and draw

my bow on them just to see them run. That was all the real enjoyment I had. I would kill deer, put them on my pony, ride up to the gate, dismount and leave the horse and deer there. If anybody wanted the deer they had to go and skin and clean them, I would not. Somebody had to stake my pony, too, for I thought work of that kind was for the squaws. I was furious if they failed to roast me the short ribs or tenderloins, but my people tried to do everything to please me for several months and I began to learn how to behave.

I would try to run away, but Willie would bring me back and the women would cry around me. I did not like tears.

At last the kindness, tenderness, and gentleness of my good Christian mother, the affectionate love of my sisters, and the vigilance of my brothers gradually wove a net of love around me that is as lasting as time itself.

Crowds would gather around to see what they called the Indian boy. I would jump on the wildest horse as he ran by me without either bridle or saddle. I would cut many capers to delight them. One day while I was amusing a crowd of spectators I noticed that they did not seem to take much interest in my performances, but gradually began to leave. I discovered that the center of attraction was down on the creek, a short distance away. I could hear talking, singing, shouting, crying, and other sounds, and I noticed everybody wore different clothes on that day. Men and women with fine clothes were going down there, and soon two or three men wearing long black coats passed me and followed the crowd. Everybody respected those fellows, and I decided they were the medicine men. I resolved to see what was going on down there, so I slipped through the bushes and watched them. I saw one of the men whom I thought was a medicine man get up and read something out of a book; occasionally he would look at his congregation and then up, and I wondered why he did not smoke; then I concluded it was a council of war, but there were too many squaws there for that. The audience rose and sang, then they all got down on their knees and covered up their faces; some groaned while others wept, and one man mumbled a lot of words; then they all got up and sang a song. The medicine man came to the front and went through a long talk and gesticulations and everybody watched him. The sober-looking man with the long coat mumbled something at first, but gradually grew louder and began singing off his speech, while the tear drops trickled down his cheeks and his face wore a sad expression. His audience seemed to lean forward and drink in every word he said. He kept talking and all the people arose and commingled their voices in a mighty chorus, while the melodious strains floated on the zephyr breeze and reached my ears and seemed as a balm to the aching pains of my breaking heart. Then shouts of laughter, shrill screams, merry faces, sad-eyed spectators, some shouted, others rushed to the center and began dancing, shaking hands and general confusion reigned supreme. It was a sure-enough old fashion Methodist shouting meeting, but of course I did not know this. I thought it must be a new kind of a war dance, rain dance or some kind of a religious ceremony, so I rushed in, gave the Comanche yell, cleared several benches and landed in the midst of the revival. My manner of worship did not suit those white people and they stampeded, leaving me "monarch of all I surveyed." I gave a few more whoops and a little dance any-way, and looked around to see what had become of all the council, and I saw the big medicine man tearing along with his coat tails flapping as he headed for my mother's home.

My people never permitted me to go to another Methodist revival until I could understand English and knew how to behave myself. True, I broke up the meeting that day, but I was just as earnest, just as fervent, just as candid and sincere as the most sanctified among them, only my mode did not conform to their theories. I have seen just as much earnestness and less hypocrisy among the Indians in their worship as I ever have seen since I came among the whites.

I amused myself by making blunt arrows, and it was fun for me to plug men away off who dared me and thought I could not hit them. One day John Davis, a young man at Loyal Valley, was off about one hundred and fifty yards. He dared me to shoot at him. He turned his back and tucked his head, and zip! my arrow took him right between the shoulders, and Mr. Davis plowed the sand with his nose. In a very few minutes there was a great blue spot where the arrow struck. I shot August Jones, another young man, with an arrow that had a spike on it, and struck the top of his shoulder. Plugging hats became one of my favorite pastimes. The boys would put their hats off about a hundred yards and bet me the drinks that I could not hit them. I would get the drinks every time, and the hat trade became good in Loyal Valley. Nearly every stranger and every drummer who came along would stick up his hat and let me shoot at it; the arrow would go through it so quick that I could often win the treats for the crowd after I had shot, for they would not believe the hat was hit until they went to get it, and then on the opposite side there would be a hole torn out. One old fellow had a fine white Stetson hat which he doubled up in a small wad and put it on a stick fifty steps away. I whizzed an arrow at it and it went clear through, making as many holes as there were doubles, but the fun played out, and I became the terror to all traveling men.

CHAPTER XLIII

CIVILIZING INFLUENCES

In due course of time I learned to talk the English and German languages, and became friends with everybody in the community. The fear the little children had toward me gave place to friendship, and the older ones began to regard me as an equal in the social scale. I learned to work, and would often be hired by ranchmen and farmers there. I knew all of the old settlers, Ship Martin, the Moseleys, William Kidd, the Marschalls, the Keysers, the Langes, and others, and was related to a great many of the settlers. In 1890 I was married to Miss Fannie Light at Loyal Valley, and to us five children were born, two boys and three girls, and they are now grown and occupy places of usefulness in the world. My oldest boy, Henry, died in a U. S. army camp at Houston, Texas, during the World War. My career has been rather checkered; I have lived as a savage and as a civilized man, and while I still love my old Indian comrades, the refining influences of civilization have wrought a great change in me. When I was a savage I thirsted to kill and to steal, because I had been taught that that was the way to live; but I know now that that is wrong. I would not take human life

HERMAN LEHMANN AND FAMILY, IN 1899

now, nor would I steal. "The way of the transgressor is hard," is a saying that is true.

I am an old man now, I will soon reach the total of three score and ten years allotted to man, if death does not claim me—seventy years of wonderful experience. I have seen many changes since I came into this world, the ox-cart gave way to the horse-drawn vehicle, and the automobile has surpassed that mode of travel. Speeding railway trains, flying machines, radios, and many other wonders have come to pass. We are living in a fast age. I am glad God has spared my life and permitted me to live to see these wonderful changes. I gave reverence to Him in the only way I knew how when I was an Indian; I worship Him now after the manner of an enlightened white man.

When I look upon these great changes I marvel and wonder how it can be so. Of many of these things I am yet in ignorance; I cannot understand how the human voice can be wafted over the radio thousands of miles without the aid of wires, but it is done, for I have heard it. It is as much a mystery to me as the first telegraph line I ever saw. A party of Indians were coming down into the settlements on a raid when, at a point in the vicinity of Fort Concho, we came upon a newly constructed telegraph line. We stopped and considered it, and wondered what it meant. Each Indian had his own notion about what it was intended for, but we were all wrong. The chief said he believed it was to be a fence to be made so high that the Indians could not get through, and so we proceeded to cut it down. Coming on down into the settlements we stole some horses and went back that way with the drove, and we found the line had been rebuilt and the wire was in place again.

And the puffing locomotive and railway train were also an object of wonder, when I came back to civilization and beheld them. The first train I ever saw was while I was with the Indians, and of course we did not know what it was, and in consequence got a scare that almost drove us frantic. We had come far down into the settlements on a raid, it may have been near Austin, and one night while we were waiting in a secluded spot in a little ravine, for the moon to come up, a train came suddenly around a curve from behind a mountain and was right on us before we had time to mount our horses. That hideous monster, belching smoke and hissing steam, and with glaring lights bore down upon us at terrific speed, and we ran, scrambling over rocks and through the brush, to get away from it. It followed us for a little ways, but we thought it had lost our trail, as it went rushing on away from us. We were somewhat scattered when things became quiet, and I was uneasy for fear the awful thing had caught three of our comrades. But when we gave our agreed assembly signal the Indians came forth from their hiding places and we held a consultation. We decided to leave that region at once and not attempt to steal any horses there, for that monster might return and catch us. It was generally agreed among us that it was the Evil Spirit that was abroad, and was seeking to devour all mankind, the white folks included. When we went back to camp and told what we had seen the Indians were greatly alarmed, and the medicine man warned us to stay out of that region.

CHAPTER XLIV

OTHER CAPTIVES

I have often been asked if the Indians had other captive white children while I was with them. It must be remembered that I was with a comparatively small band of Apaches during my captivity in that tribe, and when I joined the Comanches I was thrown with a small band. These two tribes operated in bands, and it was seldom that all of them ever came together in a large body. But nearly every band had white and Mexican captive children. There were many white children and women captured in South and West Texas. I have met some of these captives since I was restored to my people. Today there are men and women among the Indians in Oklahoma whose identity has never been established, and who are classed as Indians, but they are of white parentage. Some of the captives died among the Indians, some were purchased by their people. Clinton and Jeff Smith, captured near San Antonio, Texas, were kept by the Indians about five years. Jeff was sold to the Apaches, and was recaptured in Mexico. He now lives in San Antonio. Clinton was taken from the Comanches on the reservation at Fort Sill and sent back to his father. Dot Babb, who now lives at

Amarillo, Texas, was a captive of the Comanches for several years. Frank Buckelew, now living at Medina, Texas, was a captive of the Lipans for over a year, and managed to escape from them. Adolph Korn was captured in Mason County, and spent six years with the Comanches. He died at Mason about twenty-five years ago. Rudolph Fischer was captured by Comanches in Gillespie County, and after spending several years with them, was restored to his people, but he was not content to stay. He returned to the Indians and is with them yet, and has grown quite wealthy. Malinda Cordell was captured in Llano County many years before my capture and was kept for several years. She was finally purchased from the Indians, and in 1891 was living at Menardville. Mrs. Mahala McDonald, now living at Melvin, Texas, was captured near Harper, in Gillespie County, when she was quite small, and was kept for a few years by the Indians. There were hundreds of captives in the various tribes. In this connection I want to reproduce a chapter which appeared in a book published in 1899 by Rev. J. J. Methvin, under the title of "Andele, or the Mexican-Kiowa Captive," some of the incidents of which I am quite familiar:

"Before passing on, it will be of interest to relate a series of events in this connection which took place from 1869 to 1873. Under President Grant's peace policy, Laurie Tatum, a friend, was appointed agent for the Kiowas, Comanches, and Apaches, and on July 1, 1869, undertook the duties of that office, with agency headquarters near Fort Sill.

"At that time there was one band of Comanches, the Quo-ja-les (Kwahadi), who wandered westward towards the Rocky Mountains, living on buffalo and other wild game, and who refused to report at the agency at all. In frequent raids they stole horses from Texas, and traded them to illicit traders in New Mexico for arms and ammunition. They ridiculed the other Indians for submission to the white man, and continuing their marauding expeditions, they formed a nucleus for other Indians who were warlike and restless under the white man's rule. They sent Agent Tatum word that they would never come to the agency and shake hands till the soldiers came out to fight them, and then, if they were whipped, they would come.

"They thus set at defiance all authority till the fall of 1872, when General McKenzie, following them on one of their raids in Texas, surprised them and took one hundred of their women and children and carried them away prisoners. Soon after the Quo-ja-les reported at the agency, acknowledged their defeat, expressed their readiness to submit, and asked that their women and children be returned to them.

" 'But,' said Agent Tatum, 'you must first bring all the white and Mexican captives you have in your band.'

"Perry-o-cum, the Quo-ja-les chief, did not expect such a demand, and stood in stolid silence for some minutes, but seeing the determined look on Tatum's face, he gave instruction to his band to bring in the captives.

"In a little while they brought in Adolph Korn and Clinton Smith, two Texas boys, and two others who had forgotten their names and every word of English. They remembered some incidents of their capture, and taking these as a clue, Agent Tatum advertised in the Texas and Kansas papers and at last found their parents. Their names proved to be Temple Friend and Valentine Maxie. Twelve captive Mexicans were also thus rescued, and one case, that of little Presleano, was of special interest.

"There was an air of superiority about him. He was bright, talkative, quick to apprehend, and sprightly in movement. He seemed to have been a pet in the home and heart of old Perry-o-cum, the chief, and the boy loved the chief. Perry-o-cum knew that, and felt sure that if it was left to the choice of the boy he would not be forced to give him up. So Perry-o-cum spoke up thus:

" 'Agent Tatum, I am willing to give up all these other prisoners. It is right that I should, and you have a right to demand it, for they belong to your nation. But this boy is a Mexican, captured in Mexico, and he does not belong to your government, and you have no special right to him. I love him as my own son, and he loves me. I cannot part from him, and I know he wants to remain with me. If you will not force him away, but leave it to his own choice, I shall be satisfied.'

"Tatum watched the intense anxiety of Perry-o-cum as he spoke, and waited a little while before he replied. At last he said:

" 'Perry-o-cum, what you say is good as to giving the boy his choice, and if you will let him remain here till afternoon we will find out what is his choice.' This was readily agreed to, and the chief went away, leaving the boy in the agent's office.

The agent had a good dinner prepared, of which the boy partook with much relish, and while he was feeling particularly comfortable from the surroundings, and kindness shown him, the chief was summoned to the office again. A Mexican interpreter had been secured, and after petting the boy a while, Tatum began talking to him about his father and mother, not knowing they were dead, and that the little boy had no memory of any father and mother save old Perry-o-cum and his wife. So when he put the question, 'Do you wish to remain with Perry-o-cum, or do you want to go back to your own people?' to the delight of Perry-o-cum, he said he wanted to remain with him.

" 'But don't you want to see your brothers and sisters? Don't you want to go to them?'

"The little boy dropped his eyes in thoughtfulness a moment. The memories of home began to dawn upon him, and when he looked up again he said slowly and with a serious look upon his face, 'I want to go home.'

" 'Then I will send you,' said Agent Tatum, and as he looked across the room at Perry-o-cum, he saw the tears chasing each other down his otherwise stolid cheeks, but he was caught in his own proposition and he felt he must submit. The boy was returned to his people in Mexico through General Augur, commander of the military post at San Antonio.

"On July 10, 1870, a band of Kiowas went to the home of Gottlieb Koozer, in Texas. Mr. Koozer was not aware of the Indians' approach till he saw them in the yard, and being defenseless, he decided it was best to show a friendly spirit toward them, so he went out to meet them and offered his hand in friendship. Two of them took hold of his hands at the same time in apparent friendship, while another, stepping a little to one side, shot him through the heart. They scalped him and then went into the house, destroyed what they found therein, dresses, feather beds and many other things. They took Mrs. Koozer and her five children—one a young lady, one small girl, and three boys—and also a young man by the name of Martin Kilgore, who was about fourteen years of age, and started back to their reservation.

"As soon as news of this outrage was received at Fort Sill, Agent Tatum determined to rescue the prisoners, and find out and punish, if possible, the depredators. He announced to the Indians what he had heard, and declared that he would never issue any more government supplies to them till they brought the prisoners in. They demanded a ransom, for, two years before, they had been paid $1,500 each for some captives. He sent a letter to Mrs. Koozer by the hands of a trusty Indian on the 7th of August, 1870. On the 18th of August the Indians, giving up any idea of fighting, went to the agency with their wives and children.

"Whenever Indians are not expecting to fight, they take with them their wives and children everywhere they go, but when war is expected they send them all away together in care of the old men. When, therefore, women and children are in sight there is assurance of peace.

"They had two of the Koozer family, Miss Koozer and her little sister, with them. The little one, who had not seen her mother for several days, began crying, but was forced to hush. Indians do not allow their captives to cry. The soldiers became indignant, and stepped forward to take the captives, but in an instant the Indians pointed a dagger at the heart of the girls. The soldiers did not proceed further, for it meant sure and instant death to the girls. The Indians took them away, but seeing they could not change Agent Tatum from his purpose to withhold all government supplies till the prisoners were delivered, by 11 o'clock the two girls and two boys were brought in and delivered to him. A Mexican Kiowa had the mother, and he was stubborn and insisted upon a ransom, 'a mule and a carbine.'

"Having delivered the above four, the Indians called for the supplies, but were informed that all of the prisoners must be brought in first. Very soon Mrs. Koozer and the other boy were brought in; but they had left young Kilgore at their camp out many miles upon the reservation. Agent Tatum then paid the Indians $100 apiece for the captives, lest in the future they should kill all they found on their marauding expeditions instead of taking them captive. He then issued them the usual government supplies, with the understanding that he would issue no more till M. B. Kilgore was delivered to him.

"The Koozer family were a pitiable sight. Nobody can describe what Mrs. Koozer and her daughter suffered till they found some protection and relief from an Indian woman who seemed to have more than the usual influence of a woman among the Indians. Mrs. Koozer was appropriated by a Mexican Kiowa as his wife, and he was very cruel to her, trying twice to kill her, but she was each time protected by the chiefs.

"Three days later Colonel Grierson sent a detachment of soldiers to conduct Mrs. Koozer and her children to Montague, Texas, from which place she reached her home in safety. After the awful scenes of the past month and a half, what a home!

"These were the last captives for whom any ransom was ever paid. Soon after this another trial was made to extort a ransom for prisoners that utterly failed. It was about the time of the arrest of old Satanta and others. Old Wild Horse and six other Kiowa men and one woman went to Texas, murdered Mr. Lee and his wife and took captive their three children, Susan, aged sixteen; Millie, aged nine, and John, aged six. As soon as it was known at Fort Sill, Agent Tatum suspended all government issues to the Indians till the captives should be brought in.

"This was delayed by a proposed council, in which delegates from the civilized tribes were to be present. These civilized tribes hoped by their delegates to persuade the wild tribes to quit raiding and be peaceable. This council was set for July 22, 1872, at old Fort Cobb, but the Kiowas did not go there till ten days after.

"White Horse was stubborn, and declared that he did not want peace, but said that he and his young men would raid when and where they pleased. Lone Wolf said they would return the prisoners in their possession when Satanta and Big Tree were returned from the penitentiary, all the military posts removed from the reservation, and their reservation extended from the Rio Grande to the Missouri River.

"The delegates of the civilized tribes and Kicking Bird tried to pacify White Horse and Lone Wolf and other war-like Indians, but they could do but little. Agent Tatum adhered to his purpose to issue no more rations till the Lee children were brought in, and about a month later they delivered the two girls to Agent Richards at the Wichita Agency, and they were sent under care of Caddo George, a trusty Caddo, to Agent Tatum at Fort Sill. The boy was brought in two weeks later, and on the same day an older brother arrived from Texas and took them home.

These were the last captives the Kiowas ever took. It had become unprofitable and exceedingly dangerous, for, as Texas became more thickly settled, the people determined to put a stop to Indian raids, and they were ready to exterminate the war-like tribes, if necessary, to accomplish that end. The government, too, was proceeding by legal process to punish those who were guilty.

"Reference was made above to Satanta and Big Tree's imprisonment in the penitentiary. On May 23, 1871, General Sherman called at Agent Tatum's office and inquired if Tatum knew of any Indian band having gone to Texas recently. He said a party of Indians, about one hundred and fifty in number, had attacked a wagon train of ten wagons, seventeen miles from Fort Richardson, killing the trainmaster and six teamsters. Five escaped. He gave orders for McKenzie, with all available troops at Fort Richardson, to follow them with thirty days' rations, but as yet he had heard nothing from the pursuit.

"Tatum knew nothing, but said that he thought he could find out in a few days. Four days later the Indians came to the agency for rations, and Agent Tatum invited the chiefs into his office. He told them of the tragedy reported to him by General Sherman, and asked if they knew anything about it, that he relied upon them for the truth, and was sure that they would tell him. Satanta, after a moment's silence, arose, and in the spirit of arrogance and fiendish hate, thus addressed the agent:

" 'Yes, I led that raid. I have been told that you have stolen a large amount of our annuity goods and given them to the Texans. I have repeatedly asked for arms and ammunition which have not been furnished, and made other requests which have not been granted. You do not listen to my talk. The white people are preparing to build a railroad through our country, which will not be permitted. Some years ago we were taken by our locks and forcibly pulled here close to Texas, where we have to fight the Texas man. Some years ago, you remember, General Custer ordered me arrested and placed in prison for several days. The memory of that outrage rankles in my soul till now, and will till the last white man goes down and rots into dust again. Understand this, that no more Kiowas are ever to be arrested. On account of these grievances, a short time ago I took about a hundred of my young warriors whom I wished to train to fight, to Texas, with the chiefs, Satank, Eagle Heart, Big Tree, Big Bow and Fast Bear. We found a mule train, which we captured. We killed seven of the men, and three of my men were killed, but I am willing to call it even, and it is not necessary to say anything further about it, except to say that we do not expect to do any more raiding this summer, but I want you to understand that I led that Texas raid, and if anyone else claims the honor of it, he will be lying, for I am the man.'

"He sat down and Satank, Big Tree and Eagle Heart, who were present, confirmed the statement. As soon as Agent Tatum could get away, he left the office, hurried to the fort and requested Colonel Grierson to arrest the six chiefs who had been participants in that raid.

"Scarcely had the order been given, when Satanta took the fort interpreter and proceeded to Colonel Grierson's office. He had heard that a big Washington chief (General Sherman) was there, and he wanted to see how he measured up with him.   He was promptly arrested.   Colonel Grierson sent for Satank and Eagle Heart.   Satank reached the office and was also arrested, and Big Tree was found just outside, and while he was being arrested Eagle Heart took the alarm and fled. Kicking Bird, who had for a long time been friendly and peaceable, plead for the release of the prisoners; but here was the opportunity of impressing a great lesson upon the Indians, and they must learn it.

A few days after these arrests Colonel McKenzie arrived from Fort Richardson. Heavy rains had obliterated the tracks of the raiders so they could not be followed, so he had pressed on to Fort Sill, believing that the marauding band came from the Kiowa tribe. The prisoners were placed in his charge, and in a few days he started with them to Texas for trial. Satank was so refractory that he was put into a wagon with two soldiers and Satanta and Big Tree into another. They were all heavily manacled. George Washington, a Caddo Indian, rode on horseback along by the wagon. This was May 28, 1871.

" 'My friend,' said Satank to George, 'I wish to send by you a little message to my people. Tell them that I am dead, I died the first day out, and my bones will be lying on the roadside. I wish my people to gather them up and take them home.'

"Satanta also sent a message: 'Tell my people to take forty-one mules that we stole from Texas to the agent, as he and Colonel Grierson requires. Don't commit any more depredations around Fort Sill or in Texas.'

"In a little while Satank began to sing his death song. He was still in sight of the post—scarcely a mile away. With his back to the guards, he slipped the shackles from his wrists by taking the skin with them. He seized a butcher knife that in some mysterious way had been concealed upon his person, and started for the guards in the front part of the wagon. He struck at one of them, but missing his body made a slight wound in his leg. Both of the guards jumped from the wagon, leaving their guns. Fortunately the guns were not loaded.

"Satank seized one and began loading, declaring it would be sweet to die if he could kill only one more paleface. But, as he was pushing in the cartridge to its place several shots from the other guards put an end to Satank's efforts. He fell from the wagon, and in about twenty minutes died in great agony, gritting his teeth in defiance to the end. By order of Colonel Grierson his body was buried at Fort Sill, but he gave the Indians the privilege of taking it up and burying it elsewhere if they chose, but they never moved it.

"Satanta and Big Tree were taken on to Jacksboro, Texas, and tried for murder. Satanta was found guilty and sentenced to be hanged, but his sentence was commuted to life imprisonment. He entered the Texas penitentiary November 2, 1871. Upon recommendation of President Grant, Governor Davis of Texas let Satanta out August 9, 1873, upon parole, conditioned upon good behavior. He violated his parole and was rearrested by General Sheridan and sent back to the penitentiary November 8, 1873. After five years of a reticent, stoical life in the penitentiary, he committed suicide October 11, 1878, by jumping out of a second-story window of the prison hospital."

CHAPTER XLV

A MEMBER OF QUANAH PARKER'S FAMILY

In places in this book I have made reference to Quanah Parker, the well known Comanche chief, who was my friend, and who in many ways proved that he was my friend. When he induced the Comanche to go on the reservation the band I was with held out for a long time and would not consent to go in; he finally persuaded these Indians to go to Fort Sill and give up, and receive allotments, but I was obstinate and would not go to the post. As stated elsewhere in this book, Quanah sent me to his camp, where I stayed in fancied concealment. In the year 1877 I was adopted into Quanah Parker's family. I was seventeen years old at the time, but at that age a young Indian buck is considered a grown man. Mr. Clarke, the government agent at that time, issued government rations to Quanah Parker for my maintenance as his (Quanah's) child. I lived with Quanah's family for three years, or until I was brought home to my own people by the soldiers. I am still considered a member of Quanah Parker's family, and am recognized as such by Quanah's squaws and children, who bestowed upon me all of the affection and kindness given a full blood brother.

CHAPTER XLVI

CONCLUSION

I have now given the reader the story of my life, which has been so eventful. There are many little incidents and details which have been omitted, because if they were all told it would require a book many times the size of this volume. Enough has been told, however, to give the reader an insight in the manners and customs of the Comanche and Apache tribes of Indians. I was one of them, and I have told the story truthfully. There may be some people who think I am an impostor, or that I have never been a captive, so I am giving below a letter written by the Commissioner of Indian Affairs at Washington, D. C., in 1901, to the United States Indian Agent of the Kiowa Agency, Oklahoma, which established my identity and caused me to be enrolled as a member of the Comanche tribe, the same as if a member by blood. This should set at rest all suspicion that I may be an impostor. I have other documents to prove my identity, and I have living near me at Grandfield, Oklahoma, many old Indian comrades who regard me as a blood brother.

The letter follows:

CHAPTER XLVI

Department of the Interior,
Office of Indian Affairs,
Washington, September 30, 1901.

Lt. Col. J. F. Randlett, U. S. Indian Agent, Kiowa Agency, Okla.

Sir: Referring to your communication of the 25th ultimo, and to previous correspondence relative to the application of Herman Lehman for enrollment by adoption and full tribal rights with the Comanche Indians of the agency under your charge, you are informed that this office is now in receipt of a letter dated the 26th instant from the Acting Secretary of the Interior who decides that the said applicant is not entitled to an allotment of land with said tribe, but adds "as the Indians in 'business council' through their chiefs and headmen voted 'that he be enrolled with the Comanches, with full rights as a member of the Comanche tribe,' the Department authorizes the enrollment of the said Herman Lehman, or 'Montechema,' as a member of the Comanche tribe, entitled to all the benefits of money conferred by the agreement of October 21, 1892, the same as if a member by blood, this being the only right that the Indians could confer on persons adopted or enrolled after the cessation of their lands under the above mentioned agreement."

CONCLUSION

For your full information in the premises, I enclose herewith a copy of said decision of the Department, and you will in accordance therewith enroll the said Herman Lehman as a member of the Comanche tribe of Indians, and advise all persons interested of your action in the matter.

Mr. R. N. Richardson, the atty. in the case, has this day been informed of the action of the Department, and furnished a copy of said decision.

Very respectfully,

A. C. TONNER,

Acting Commissioner.

My mother died at Castell, Texas, in 1912, at a very old age; my brother Willie, who was captured by the Apaches at the same time I was captured, and who escaped from them a few days later, lives near Loyal Valley, Texas, yet, and has a good ranch property there; another brother, Adolph Lehmann, lives in Menard County, Texas, and is in good circumstances; my sister, Mrs. Mina Keyser, lives at Loyal Valley, and my sister, Caroline, lives in Dallas. To the dear old mother, and to these noble brothers and sisters I owe all for my restoration, for if it had not been for them I would today be an Indian still.